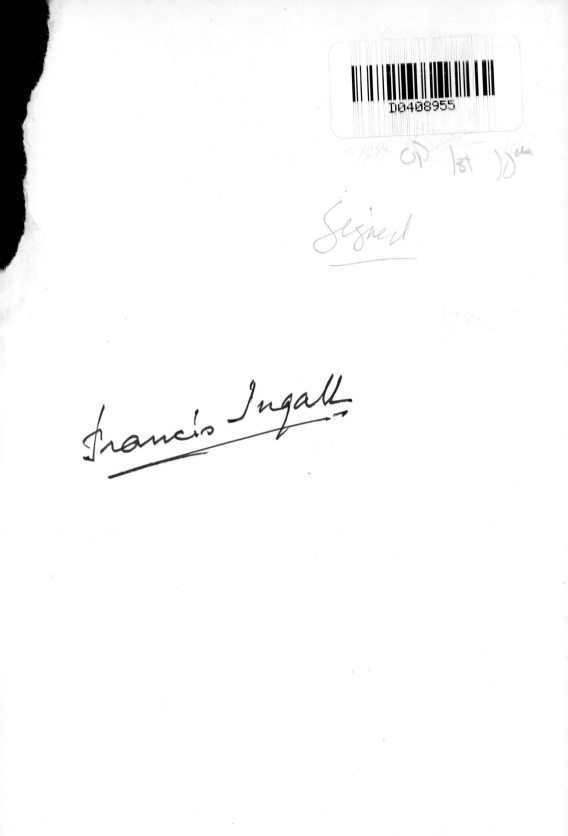

Signed

Francis Ingall

THE
LAST OF THE
BENGAL LANCERS

THE LAST OF THE BENGAL LANCERS

Francis Ingall

PRESIDIO

Published 1988 by Presidio Press
31 Pamaron Way, Novato CA 94949

Copyright © 1988 by Francis Ingall
Published in Great Britian 1988 by Leo Cooper Ltd

LIBRARY OF CONGRESS
Library of Congress Cataloging-in-Publication Data

Ingall, Francis, 1908-
    The last of the Bengal Lancers / Francis Ingall.
      p.   cm.
    Includes index
    ISBN 0-89141-203-4
    1. Ingall, Francis, 1908-   . 2. World War, 1939-1945--India.
    3. Great Britain. Army--Biography. 4. Generals--Great Britain-
    -Biography. 5. Great Britain. Army. Duke of Connaught's Own
    Lancers, 6th--History. I. Title.
    D767.6.I59 1988
    940.54' 12' 410924--dc19
    [B]   88-26584
                                                                CIP

Printed in the United States of America

To my charger Eagerhart

and all the brave cavalry horses

Contents

Illustrations

Foreword

The images of the Raj evoked in Brigadier Ingall's memoirs will delight not only many of an earlier generation who served in British India, but also a younger audience enamoured by the grandeur and idiosyncracies of a bygone era. The author's formidable knowledge and deep understanding of the people and their traditions enable him to write with the grace and ease borne of familiarity. In a web of tales encompassing interesting events and charming encounters, Ingall brings to life this fascinating period in the history of the sub-continent.

Ingall's rich and varied experiences span the pre-independence era to the formative phase of Pakistan's development when he was called upon by Jinnah to establish the Pakistan Military Academy in 1947 – an achievement for which he was awarded an OBE by King George VI. The latter part of the book focuses on the establishment of the Pakistan Military Academy which is today recognized as one of the finest institutions of its kind in the developing world.

It was while Brigadier Ingall was Commandant at the PMA (1947–1951) that I had the good fortune to have been a cadet. He inspired us with his love of independence and spirit of adventure which is so candidly reflected in his book. The Pakistan Army will always remain greatly indebted to him. *The Last of the Bengal Lancers* is a fine specimen of its genre and will no doubt be appreciated by all those interested in the Raj and its immediate aftermath.

(Ejaz Azim)
Ambassador of Pakistan
to the United States

9 September, 1986

Reveille

Cavalry trumpets with their flat blare have always appealed to me more than the bugle's shrill demand.

I was sleeping peacefully in my camp cot when I was awakened by reveille sounded by the massed trumpeters of the 6th Duke of Connaught's Own Bengal Lancers. As I turned over, my orderly presented me with a mug of steaming tea and some shaving water. Outside I could hear the stamping and snorting of six hundred horses, heaving themselves to their feet as their riders prepared them for the day's action.

The regiment was encamped at Bara Fort, ten miles from Peshawar, at the edge of the Kajauri Plain. The month was October, 1930, and already the promise of the cold weather was apparent. Mist was rising from the river and there was a nip in the air. The rising sun, already tinting the swaying tops of the sugar cane, illuminated the stark tribal-occupied mountains to the west.

I shaved and washed, donned my breeches and boots and repaired outside my tent to have my khaki *pagri* (turban) tied around my head by my orderly.

As soon as the horses were groomed, watered and fed, the men and officers gathered for a quick meal before moving out of camp. Everyone was aware of the overall plan as the CO had briefed us all the previous evening. The officers in turn had explained our job to the *sowars* (troopers) and we had settled down for the night.

Such was the routine beginning of the day when first I went into battle, riding forth on my charger, sword in hand, much as my predecessors had done at the battle of Tel-el-Kebir in 1882.

1

The Bengal Lancers

What is a Bengal Lancer? To explain fully, it is necessary to go back to the beginning of the Indian Army, to the days when it was a private army, owned and paid for by the East India Company. After the Mutiny this private army became an Imperial force comprising three administrative armies in India: the Bengal Army, the Madras Army and the Bombay Army. There were also a few lesser contingents such as the Hyderabad Contingent, the Central India Horse and the Frontier Force in the Punjab.

Of the cavalry, the majority of regiments in the Bengal Army were lancers; hence they became known as 'Bengal Lancers'. These units did not necessarily serve only in the Presidency of Bengal; they were stationed all over India. In the course of time they served all over the world.

My regiment was formed in 1857; or more correctly, the two regiments that were the ancestral units of my regiments were formed in 1857–8. These were the 13th and 16th Bengal Lancers. They changed their names and their titles several times throughout their existence. At one time the 16th was known as the 16th Bengal Cavalry; at another it was known simply as the 16th Cavalry. The 13th Bengal Lancers, on the other hand, retained that basic title throughout its history.

There is a humorous story concerning the title of the 13th. In 1882 the Regiment joined the British forces in Egypt. At the battle of Tel-el-Kebir the Egyptian Army was soundly trounced by the British. The 13th Bengal Lancers took part in a highly successful charge on that day and this action was observed by His Royal Highness the Duke of Connaught, the youngest son of Queen Victoria, who was then commanding the 1st Guards Brigade with the Expeditionary Forces. When the battle was over, he said to the Lieutenant-Colonel commanding the Regiment, 'Colonel, I congratulate you. I am going to ask Her Majesty that I be appointed Colonel-in-Chief of your Regiment. In future, you will be known as the 13th Duke of Connaught's Own Bengal Lancers.' Well, the Colonel didn't go for fancy titles at all and he thought that '13th Bengal Lancers' was sufficiently distinguished for him or anybody else. He had the temerity, so history relates, to say that he didn't wish to have his Regiment known as the Duke of Connaught's anything!

But Her Majesty at Windsor decided otherwise; the Duke was duly appointed. On his return to India the Colonel complained to Army HQ and argued that, while he would of course accept HRH as the Colonel-in-Chief, there was no need to encumber the Regiment with a fancy title. He must have had some influence. In subsequent army lists the 13th appeared as 'The Duke of Connaught's', the possessive 'Own' being omitted.

If the student of the history of the Indian Army is confused by royal titles it is understandable. Another regiment, the 31st Bombay Lancers, was also awarded the title of 'Duke of Connaught's Own' for their part in another action at a later date, 1890. They were known as the *Duke of Connaught's Own* while the 13th continued to be known as the 13th *Duke of Connaught's* Bengal Lancers.

This is even more confusing to people looking through the Army List because in 1921, when the size of the British and Indian Armies was reduced, many regiments were amalgamated – including the 13th and 16th Bengal Lancers, which were thereafter known as the 6th Duke of Connaught's *Own* Lancers. At the same time, the 31st and 32nd Bombay Lancers were merged to form the *new* 13th Duke of Connaught's *Own* Lancers.

It was to the 6th Duke of Connaught's Own Lancers that I was gazetted in 1930. Strictly speaking, from 1921 onwards there were no longer any regiments with the name 'Bengal' in their title, but those lancer regiments who traced their origin to the old Bengal Army were often referred to as 'Bengal Lancers'.

When my Regiment went to the Middle East and Europe during the Second World War, the press always referred to us as 'a famous regiment of Bengal Lancers'. I suppose they thought they were doing the right thing as far as security was concerned, but I'm quite sure the Germans knew our full title anyway.

To return to the question: what is a Bengal Lancer? In my view, although there were many fellows who joined my own Regiment from civilian life during the Second World War, and served with distinction, they were not Bengal Lancers in the true sense of the term. In other words, when I joined

2

my Regiment in 1930, the Regiment was horses, the *sowars* (troopers, enlisted men) carried lances, and the officers carried sabres and pistols. The Regiment had the same sort of organization and was doing the same sort of job as the 13th Bengal Lancers were doing when first raised in 1857. Later, of course, that changed. In 1940 the 6th Lancers was mechanized and became a light armoured regiment, reorganized and re-equipped to play a distinguished part in the Second World War.

With the passing of the horse, an era ended. The Bengal Lancer officer, mounted on his charger with sword in hand, had become an anachronism. As an officer who served in the 'horse days' and took part in mounted action, I can claim to be one of the last of the Bengal Lancers in the traditional sense.

How does a lancer regiment differ from other cavalry regiments? Strictly speaking, there are few differences. In a general way, all mounted units can be called cavalry and the horsed regiments of the Indian Army were referred to overall as the Indian Cavalry. This was true despite some variation in the regiments; some carried sabres while others were equipped with lances.

When I joined in 1930, there were twenty-one Indian cavalry regiments, all with different titles. There was the 1st Duke of York's Own Lancers (Skinner's Horse – so named for James Skinner who raised the Regiment). For a similar reason, the 2nd Royal Lancers was called Gardner's Horse; and my own Regiment, the 6th Duke of Connaught's Own Lancers, also had a secondary title, Watson's Horse, the 13th Bengal Lancers having been raised in 1858 by General John Watson VC.

Technically all Indian cavalry regiments were light cavalry. In the nineteenth century there were two types, light and heavy. The light cavalry were all lancers and hussars. They had lighter horses, lighter equipment, smaller men and carried a lesser load. They were the eyes of the army, performing duties that were later performed by reconnaissance units or armoured car regiments. Their primary job was not shock action, although the Charge of the Light Brigade at Balaclava is a famous exception. Other regiments were heavy cavalry: dragoons, dragoon guards and life guards. They had bigger horses and bigger men who were armed with a heavy sabre. They were the shock troops of horsed cavalry days. All were armed with a cutting sabre in the days of Balaclava and Waterloo, but in 1910 our cavalry regiments were issued with what is known as the pointing sabre – a sword with a very sharp point at the end of a blunt blade. The idea was that you skewered your opponent as opposed to cutting his head off!

Despite – or perhaps because of – our Regiment's lengthy title, for general purposes we were referred to as '6th Lancers'. On our shoulders we wore simply '6L'. All the enlisted men were Indian and all the officers were

3

British. This was not necessarily the case in other cavalry regiments, some of which had a proportion of Indian officers while others were wholly Indian (I refer to Indian officers holding the King's commission, as opposed to the Viceroy's commission; the latter were known as warrant officers). In my day the entire complement of officers in the 6th Lancers was British. Our complement was twelve officers, but all regiments had more than that figure, because a number of officers officially borne on the strength of the regiment were absent on extra-regimental duty.

When I joined, the 6th Lancers had twenty officers on the Regimental List. One of those in extra-regimental employ was Mo Mayne who became a famous general in the Second World War – he took the surrender of the Duke of Aosta in Abyssinia, was later promoted full general and knighted. Mo, when I joined the Regiment, was a brevet lieutenant-colonel, but was shown in the Army List as squadron commander; he wasn't even second-in-command of the Regiment, being too junior in length of service. He was away on a staff job. The authorized twelve comprised the Officer Commanding (referred to as 'the Colonel'), the Second-in-Command, the Adjutant, the Quartermaster, and the various squadron commanders and squadron officers. Most young officers had to take a turn as Quartermaster, while the Adjutant, nominated by the CO, was considered a key appointment.

There were three Lancer Squadrons and one Headquarters Squadron. We were a 'class composition' Regiment – and that needs explaining.

Prior to 1857, the year of the Indian Mutiny, the soldiers of most regiments were all of one class: all Muslims or all Hindus. To incite the sepoys (Indian Soldiers) to revolt, troublemakers began to plant rumours that government-issued rifle bullets were smeared with either pig's fat or cow's fat. To prepare the cartridge for firing, a sepoy had to break one end of it with his teeth. Thus, a Muslim regiment was fed the story that it was pig's fat – and the pig, of course, is anathema to any Muslim since he considered it unclean; if he eats of the pig, when he dies he goes straight to Gehenna (hell) and suffers the torment of the damned. Hindu regiments, on the other hand, were told that the cartridge was smeared with cow's fat – and Hindus venerate the cow. The story spread rapidly through the ranks because everybody was of the same religious persuasion.

After the Mutiny, following the principle of 'divide and rule', the British started what they called 'class composition' regiments, mixing two or more different races or religions in each unit. The theory was that any unrest within one particular faction would become known to another (presumably unsympathetic) group, which would then spill the beans.

The 6th Lancers was one such composite Regiment. When I joined, one Lancer Squadron consisted of Muslims, one of Hindus and one of Sikhs;

4

Headquarters Squadron was a conglomeration of all three. The Lancer Squadrons each had four troops of approximately thirty-five men each. Each troop was commanded by what in those days we called an 'Indian officer' (IO as opposed to BO), who later became known as a 'Viceroy's Commissioned Officer' – a warrant officer, in fact. He did not have the powers of a British officer, and never sat on courts martial for instance, but he did have considerable powers within the Regiment. He had risen from the ranks, having started as an enlisted trooper or *sowar*, then become an NCO and later, if he were an outstanding man, become what we termed an 'Indian officer'.

There were two grades of 'Indian officer' in the cavalry: the junior was the *jemadar*, with one star on his shoulder; the other was the *risaldar*, who rated two stars. Over and above all of the Indian ranks was the *risaldar*-major who was a sort of super, super sergeant-major, as one might say in British terms. He wore a crown on his shoulder similar to a major's. Their badges of rank were slightly different to those worn by BOs and later, when they were renamed 'Viceroy's Commissioned Officers', they wore a little braid underneath their badges of rank. These were the men who commanded the 'troops', or platoons in infantry parlance.

As I have said, there were four troops in each Lancer Squadron with three sections in each troops. Sections were commanded by an NCO, either a two-striper or three-striper. These NCOs had special titles also: they were not called corporals, lance-corporals or sergeants as in the British Army. In the cavalry, a one-striper was called acting lance-*duffadar*, the two-striper lance-*duffadar* and the three-striper was a *duffadar*. He was the senior chap in the troop. Each squadron had a *duffadar*-major, the equivalent of a sergeant-major, and also a quartermaster-*duffadar*, like a quartermaster-sergeant in British terms. The overall pattern was much the same as the British Army.

When I joined the 6th Lancers we had no light automatic weapons at all, but in addition to the lance the men were armed with the .303 Lee-Enfield rifle which was carried in a 'bucket' at the back of the saddle, a sort of large leather scabbard which looked rather like an umbrella stand. The lance, of course, was carried by the man in his right hand. On the edge of the stirrup iron in which his foot rested was another 'bucket', a small leather egg-cup which supported the butt of the lance when the man was at rest or at attention. If he wanted to use the lance offensively, he pulled it out of the bucket, holding it in his right hand. He was able to use either the butt or the point, depending on the situation.

About three or four years later, each troop had a light machine gun carried on a packhorse. Rejoicing in the name of the Vickers-Berthier, or VB for short, this type of LMG was a forerunner of the Bren gun and somewhat similar to it. Cavalry never had the Lewis gun with which the British infantry had been armed in the First World War and still was when I joined the Army in 1930. A horrendous gun, I seem to remember it had 330 working parts and 340 stoppages! The VB was simplicity itself. The first VB gun course, at the Machine Gun School, Ahmednagar, in the south of India, was attended by a representative officer from each cavalry regiment in India and I was the 6th Lancers' representative. We did not take the course very seriously, not being enthusiastic about the advent of a light machine gun for cavalry. Most of us felt that our job in wartime was reconnaissance and that the introduction of more sophisticated weapons, needing packhorses, etc., would reduce our mobility. But we had a lot of fun, not only in Ahmednagar but also in nearby Poona and Bombay, and the bridge in the mess was excellent.

The Headquarters Squadron was the administrative unit of the Regiment. In addition to the quartermaster's empire, there was a signal troop and a medium machine-gun troop, the farrier major and a mobile forge. The main basis of the Regiment's firepower was the MG (machine-gun) troop, which had four Vickers guns. These medium machine guns had been used by the British Army with a great deal of success since the Boer War. The Vickers was a marvellous gun. I think it had ten working parts and had practically no stoppages at all; it would just go on firing for ever. With a water-cooled jacket and a belt which carried the ammunition out of a box, it was one of the most reliable automatic MGs ever invented. In the MG troop they were carried on packhorses; one horse carried the gun and the tripod, and another the ammunition and accessories, including a Barr & Stroud range-finder.

The Vickers itself was similar to the US Army's Browning machine gun, but was not so precise. The Vickers had a particularly large effective beaten zone (EBZ). When the gun was fired, the muzzle oscillated up and down so that the 'fall of shot' was spread over a wide area. It was not designed to be a precise weapon at all and produced a sort of 'scatter-gun' effect. It was quite accurate laterally; it didn't wander right and left of a given target. You could set it to automatic traverse and it would spray bullets back and forth over the whole target area. It was a fine gun and really was our only artillery, since we had no mortars or anything of that nature.

In the signal troop the men had a flag with which they transmitted the Morse code, a more comprehensive method than semaphore. They also had a heliograph, which had been in use about a hundred years. This was a very intricate and attractive piece of equipment: a mirror which picked up rays of the sun and projected them towards your friends receiving the message. It had a key for sending the Morse code in flashes that could be seen over great distances. In addition to the heliograph, the signallers had lamps which

6

operated with a key on the same principle. Inside the lamp was an aiming device and a bulb. It was powered by a separate battery, which was rather a bulky thing to cart around, but the signaller was able to buzz the key up and down in the same way a telegraphist once did in a railway station. The light went on and off and the person at the other end could see this from quite some distance away. The heliograph was probably more distinct over greater distances. Such was the communication equipment we used to pass messages.

In addition, of course, written or verbal messages could be sent by galloper – a method not much changed since Captain Nolan attempted to contact Lord Cardigan at Balaclava, nearly eighty years before. While on the subject of the Charge of the Light Brigade at Balaclava (1854), even in my day all young cavalry officers were imbued with what was commonly known as 'the cavalry spirit'; in other words: *If in doubt – charge!* That may sound somewhat crude, but some of the greatest military disasters have been caused by a commander sitting inert on his backside while events overwhelmed him and his troops. History also relates that quick action by a forceful character can turn defeat into victory, even in the face of great odds.

The total strength of the Regiment was about 600 men and horses. Incidentally, in the British and Indian Armies, cavalry was always referred to as a 'regiment' as opposed to a 'battalion'. An infantry regiment might have had five or six battalions, which were part of the regiment as a whole, quite a different organization to the cavalry regiment. Artillery also used different terms; for instance, there were generally three batteries of artillery in an artillery brigade. Later, the term 'regiment' was substituted for 'brigade', but only as far as artillery was concerned. It can be very confusing, even for those of us who had the privilege to serve in the Army in those days – whether we belonged to a regiment, battalion or brigade.

2

Early Days and Sandhurst

The man who first told me about life in India and whetted my appetite to become a Bengal Lancer was Colonel C. O. Harvey of the Central India Horse. 'C. O.', as he was known, was Military Secretary to the Viceroy of India for many years and at the beginning of the Second World War he was the first divisional commander of the division in which I served, the 8th Indian Division. It was sheer chance that I happened to meet C. O. through a cousin in the Royal Navy, at a time when I was considering which cavalry regiment to approach. But this chance meeting was to seal my fate.

I was born on 24 October, 1908, at my father's house, Invermark, on the fringe of Limpsfield Common in the county of Surrey, England. My father was a member of the London Stock Exchange, being the senior partner in F. D. Ingall & Co. We can trace our direct descent back to the middle of the sixteenth century; accurate names and dates do not exist prior to that time, but there is strong evidence to suggest that our antecedents were sea rovers from Uppsala in Sweden, who founded a settlement at Fortingall in what is now Perthshire round about the year AD 960. Part of the clan moved south and settled at Ingleton in Yorkshire for some hundreds of years; then, sometime in the sixteenth century, one branch of the family moved further afield, to Skirbeck in Lincolnshire. It was this branch that provided some of the early settlers in America: two brothers, Edmund and Francis Ingall, are believed to have founded the town of Lynn, Massachusetts. At about this time the American branch added an 's' to their patronymic.

I sometimes wonder whether I inherited my love for the Army from my great-grandfather, Tankerville Chamberlain Drew, who was commissioned into HM 45th Foot in 1810 and fought under the Duke of Wellington in the Peninsular Campaign. A miniature portrait shows a distinct resemblance between this ancestor and myself. During the next hundred years a number of the family distinguished themselves as soldiers, the most notable being Frederick Lenox, who served in HM 15th Regiment of Foot and retired as a general. But of my immediate family none were professional army officers, although during the First World War my eldest brother, Bruce Barclay, served in the 1st Battalion The Gordon Highlanders and in the Second World War my second brother, Ivor Barclay, in the Royal Air Force. Alas, both have now departed.

When my parents at last got the message that I was determined to make the Army my career, my mother – who was Scottish – wanted me to follow my brother into the Gordons. I would have been proud to have entered this very distinguished regiment, but the great love of my life was horses; I would only go into the cavalry. So there was a lot of talk about cavalry regiments and which one should be approached. This was when I had the good fortune of meeting Colonel Harvey and decided that my future lay with the Bengal Lancers. He recommended that I should request a posting to the 6th Duke of Connaught's Own Lancers.

The year was 1926. My housemaster at Hurstpierpoint was told to enter my name for the Royal Military College at Sandhurst. Unfortunately I had an accident, got septic pleurisy and damn near died. While I was in hospital and still feeling pretty groggy, my housemaster came to visit me. He was a priest and evidently knew that it was touch-and-go with me, for he launched into a pompous talk about life and death, at the end of which he said: 'My boy, if you go, I know you will go like a sportsman and gentleman.'

Since that time I have seen my share of death and in no way would I describe it as either sporting or gentle. Even then, feeling as ill as I did, I laughed out loud. From that moment on I started to mend and was able to pass the Sandhurst medical the next year with flying colours.

My accident did have one advantage, however. Being away from school for some months had affected my academic studies, so the school arranged for me to receive a nomination to the Royal Military College. I had never been a very brilliant scholar, and this arrangement came as a welcome surprise; although I still had to sit the entrance examination, I knew that whatever my results I would be accepted anyway.

With my name being put forward for nomination I had to have two sponsors. My father asked two old friends of the family to vouch for me, Sir Edward Clarke and Sir Maurice (later Lord) Hankey. Sir Maurice had been Secretary to the Cabinet for many years and had considerable influence in various circles; he also knew certain members of the Royal Family. This was to prove invaluable as the Duke of Connaught was, of course, Colonel-in-

Chief of the regiment that Colonel Harvey had recommended. Sir Maurice arranged for me to be received by His Royal Highness, and thus the wheels were set in motion.

Arriving at Sandhurst on a rather drab afternoon in the late summer of 1927, I was directed to report to 5 Company – 'lovely Five' as it was known – and duly found my way to the company's colonnaded portals, along with dozens of other new cadets.

At Sandhurst we glorified in the title of 'gentlemen cadets'; every drill instructor had to call us 'Mister' or 'Sir' even if he were about to punish us. Most of us came from the British public schools. So far from being 'public' these schools are exclusively private, all tuition fees, board and lodging being paid by the boy's parents. In my day, a few selected soldiers came from the ranks (enlisted men) of the Army; classified as 'Y' cadets, all their tuition fees and keep was paid by the Government. Most of them were outstanding soldiers and one who was there in my term became a very distinguished general. My father had to pay for the whole of my education at Sandhurst, a basic one thousand pounds a year – quite a substantial sum in those days – as well as meet the cost of all my uniforms and equipment and also give me an allowance. But this has all changed. Nowadays a gentleman cadet's education, lodging and other necessary expenses are paid by the Ministry of Defence; in fact the cadets themselves are now paid, and they receive more today than I was paid as a second lieutenant.

In the 1920s the RMC Sandhurst trained young men for commissions in the cavalry and infantry, whereas the Royal Military Academy at Woolwich provided the intake for the Royal Artillery, Engineers and Royal Corps of Signals. Understandably there was great rivalry between the two establishments; sporting events between the two often ended in mayhem!

My first impression of Sandhurst was one of bustle. There seemed to be innumerable drill sergeants in a variety of Guards uniforms, all barking like sheep dogs.

'Come along, sir . . .'

'Hurry up, sir . . .'

'You're no longer at school, sir . . .'

'Keep moving, keep moving!'

Every waking moment of a cadet's first few months he was being chased, not only by the drill sergeants but also by a number of senior cadets, under-officers and cadet sergeants. There always seemed to be someone behind me shouting: 'Get a move on, Mr Ingall, sir! Double, sir! You're a very dozy gentleman, SIR!'

Mean and lowly juniors, we were all too conspicuous, particularly for the first month. Before our arrival we had been given a concise list of civilian clothes to bring in our trousseau. One item on this list was a pair of chocolate-coloured denim overalls which we had to wear until our uniforms had been cut and fitted by the college tailors. The denims, or 'fatigues' as they were aptly named, were stiff with starch; they chafed and rubbed all the most tender and intimate parts of one's anatomy. Another item on the list was a cloth cap, and it was marked as an absolute necessity. I wondered why; after all, one would have thought we could receive our first few weeks' training bareheaded. But I soon found out that even a lowly gentleman cadet could never be seen on parade without his headgear, and the regulations did not permit one to salute unless one wore a cap of some kind. And, of course, the life of a cadet at Sandhurst was one long salute.

Our first six weeks seemed to be spent entirely on the drill square. The standard of foot and rifle drill was certainly the highest in the British Army, perhaps in the world. Often selected parties of cadets were sent to demonstrate drill to regular army battalions. The head of the drill staff in 5 Company was Sergeant-Major Bill Manger of the Coldstream Guards. He had a bristly walrus moustache and his Coldstream cap, with a white band and gold lines on its peak, always lay flat on his nose. He carried a pacestick under his left arm, effectively the badge of office of the elite drill instructors, for no other category of instructor carried one. A pacestick is a wooden implement which opens up like a caliper to measure the accuracy of a squad's paces, the length of a pace for Infantry of the Line being a regulation thirty inches.

Most of the cadets undergoing this rigorous indoctrination were prepared to accept almost any indignity to achieve their chosen goal, a commission in His Majesty's Land Forces. But this wasn't always the case. A few were there simply because their family had insisted they take up an army career, not because they had any real desire to become officers or had any aptitude for the soldier's life. Under the increasing pressure some just faded and quietly disappeared; one day they were there, the next they had vanished and were forgotten. Others went rather less quietly – like George Elsner. A delightful chap, George apparently had no intention of completing the course; he certainly gave an excellent impression of wishing to be elsewhere than at Sandhurst, and hardly a day passed when he was not placed on a charge of some sort.

I well remember one day when George caused havoc on the parade ground. On our very first parade Sergeant-Major Manger had marched up and down our ranks asking each cadet his name and we all had to answer in the correct manner: 'Ingall, Staff.' (All NCO or warrant officer instructors were addressed as 'Staff'.) But Manger repeated the performance day after day for the first couple of weeks, even though he had long since memorized the names of the whole squad. One day he was walking down the front rank

11

asking his usual question, 'What's your name, sir?', and eliciting the usual response from each cadet. We all stood rigid, eyes to the front, anxious for the Sergeant-Major's approval. All, that is, save one man. Just as Bill Manger asked his question for the second or third time, a loud voice said: 'That's a lot of bullshit!'

I recognized the voice as George Elsner's, standing in the middle of the rear rank.

The Sergeant-Major's cap almost fell off. *'Who said that?'* he roared.

'I did, Staff,' said George.

'Oh you did, did you? Well, goddammit, sir – one pace backwards *march!*' The Sergeant-Major doubled round the end of the rank towards his victim. But no way was George going to move. So: 'You're under arrest, Mr Elsner, sir!'

Manger pointed to the cadets either side of George and ordered them to escort him off the parade ground to the guardroom. The poor fellow on George's left didn't move smartly enough and he ended up in the 'pokey' too. The rest of us stood in silence as we watched, shaking with a mixture of suppressed laughter and awe.

Eventually George Elsner got his way and left the RMC for good. Alas, I do not know what happened to him. Probably he was overtaken by the Second World War and willy-nilly found himself in the armed services anyway.

There were others who had no intention of making the Army a lifetime career and who merely intended to spend a few years in a fashionable regiment, then enter the family business. In this category was a good friend of mine, the baronet Sir Charles Mappin. As heir to the famous London jewellery house of Mappin & Webb, Charles had plenty of money and was never able to take army life very seriously.

At Sandhurst we all had soldier servants, one between two or three gentlemen cadets (or 'GCs' as we were called). My servant, shared with two others, was 'Uncle' Bob Bartlett. Uncle was a real character, almost a monument; he had been a servant at Sandhurst since 1913. He had an enormous paunch and to support this vast overhang he wore his belt well below his navel. In his mouth at all times was a little cut-off clay pipe, generally smoked upside down. He had about four chins and the spittle from his pipe used to dribble down the crevices of these chins before finally disappearing in some subterranean hollow. He also swore all the time; never a sentence came out of his mouth without some swear word in it – in fact I have never known a man with a greater set of expletives.

Uncle was supposed to clean our rooms and make our beds, but he was an idle old man and never did very much. He was also supposed to help us clean our equipment, which always had to be immaculate – even the slightest smear on the tip of one's bayonet brought instant retribution – but if we let him do this we were simply asking for a reprimand on parade. Unless we greased his palm; then he could produce fantastic results on a piece of leather or steel.

The only time I saw Uncle jolted out of his ponderous progression through life was early one morning when he burst into my room. It was about 5 am and I was fast asleep but he barged his way through my door with none of that 'May I come in, sir' nonsense.

'Mr Ingall, Mr Ingall, come quick!' he panted.

'Jesus, Uncle, what's the matter? Is there a fire or something?'

'No, no,' he puffed. 'Come to Sir Charles's room! Quick!'

It seemed that Charles had had an early call, so Uncle had gone to his room to wake him up as arranged.

'. . . And blow me down, there he was in bed with a great big ginger tart alongside o' him!', said Uncle.

I could hardly believe this, but I rushed out of my own room and down the passage to Charles's quarters. Sure enough, there was Charles, sitting up in bed beside a very decorative red-haired lady. Both were clearly drunk and, though she was clutching herself in a loose sort of way, I got the impression that she couldn't have cared less about her nudity. Uncle was goggle-eyed.

We had to get the lady out before parade, when snoopers came round to check on all the rooms, so I told Uncle to find a friend of mine, Bruce Seton, to help me resolve the problem. Uncle duly trotted off – I had never seen him move so fast – and returned with Bruce.

Never in my subsequent career have I had to face a more urgent situation. Bruce and I had a quick confab, then we told the lady to remove her make-up – though actually there wasn't much left on her face; Charles had done a good job on her, apparently. Meanwhile we got hold of a spare set of fatigues, a belt and a uniform cap. Fortunately the lady was not too well-endowed and when dressed, with her hair completely hidden under the cap, she looked like a rather well-developed young man. As Uncle and I were handling 'wardrobe and make-up', Bruce rounded up a few volunteers, all dressed in the same brown denim overalls, and we formed a little squad of six or eight including the lady. With me 'in charge' as I had just been promoted Cadet Lance-Corporal, we left the company building by the back entrance where we were slightly less likely to be seen and marched off down the road towards the back gate. I must admit the lady played her part well and kept in step as best she could.

On duty at the gate was one of the college policemen, retired soldiers who wore a blue uniform and thus were referred to as 'bluebottles'. The GCs would bait them mercilessly and generally do their best to embarrass them at every opportunity, so they tended to leave us 'gentlemen' alone, particularly if we looked as if we were on official business.

'Where are you going, sir?' the bluebottle asked me.

'Preparation squad for a musketry exercise, Staff.' It was sounded awfully weak, even to my ears, but the bluebottle let us pass.

As soon as we were round the corner we told the lady to beat it to one of the local hotels, where she could lie low until Charles arrived to bail her out. So off she went, while we hung around for twenty minutes to try to make our story seem more credible. Then we formed up again and marched back to the gate.

'Didn't take long, sir,' commented the bluebottle.

'Wrong place, Staff,' I blurted. 'We've got to hurry!'

And back we marched with me shouting 'Left, right, left, right' till we reached the company and disappeared into our quarters like rabbits down a burrow.

But I shall never forget Uncle's face that morning, all his chins quivering with excitement. It's been known as 'the ginger tart story' ever since.

Uncle could arrange almost anything. He soon discovered that I was mad about horses and one day when I was supposedly studying he came into my room and asked: ''Ow would you like some nice quiet 'acking of an afternoon? It'll only cost you five bob.'

Although we had riding instruction several days a week, I could never get enough horse exercise. There were a couple of livery stables in the village of Sandhurst where one could hire a horse, either for a hack or to attend a meet of the local hunt; but they were expensive and I couldn't afford them very often on my allowance. So I immediately pricked up my ears.

'That's very interesting, Uncle. Where would I find a horse for this money?'

Uncle sucked on his pipe. 'Ask no questions and you'll be told no lies. If you want to go for a 'ack in the afternoon, you tell me in the morning and I'll arrange a 'orse and groom to meet you at Lower Star Point.'

Lower Star Point was a place where five tracks crossed in the woods at the back of Sandhurst. There were miles and miles of heathland in the area; it was beautiful wild country and a lovely place to ride a horse. So a few days later I told Uncle that I wanted to go for a hack and he made the promised arrangements.

I cycled out to Lower Star Point and found the groom there standing beside a big chestnut gelding; it was very well turned out with a nice saddle. I mounted the horse and told the groom I'd be back in a couple of hours. The horse was a beautiful ride; I enjoyed myself immensely and gladly handed the groom his five bob when I returned. He touched his cap, mounted and rode off.

This arrangement went on for months. I never inquired where the horse came from, or what the groom's name was. Then one day I rented a horse from the local stable to go hunting with the Garth Hunt, a private pack that was due to meet at the Staff College. Normally GCs were not allowed into this area, although it is within the grounds of R MC Sandhurst, as the Staff College is where captains and majors receive higher military training. But on this occasion, because of the meet, I was able to enter the exalted territory.

My hireling horse was awaiting me at the appointed time. I mounted and looked around me. To my surprise, there beside me was the very chestnut gelding I had been 'borrowing' so often of late. And on his back sat a most distinguished gentleman.

Edging away discreetly, I rode around the crowd and suddenly spotted the groom to whom I'd been giving my five bob. I asked him who was riding 'our' horse.

'Oh, didn't you know, sir?' he smirked. 'That's General X, the Staff College Commandant. It's his horse, sir.'

I damn nearly fell out of the saddle. There was I, riding the General's horse for months on end – and on grounds just behind the Staff College! We could so easily have met during one of my rides. I blushed to think of the possible consequences of such a confrontation; probably I would have been sent down, or at least, 'restricted'. But when I upbraided Uncle, all he said was: 'Wot the eye don't see, the 'eart don't grieve for!'

That was typical of Uncle; he was never overawed by authority, least of all by the Academy Adjutant who was in charge of discipline at Sandhurst – and I mean *discipline*! – not only of GCs but of soldier servants too. This, of course, included Uncle Bob Bartlett.

The Adjutant in my time was a real martinet: Captain F. A. M. Browning, Grenadier Guards, whose youthful appearance had earned him the soubriquet 'Boy'. He was extremely good-looking and I never met an officer more impeccably turned out. He also had a voice that could turn the toughest drill sergeant to jelly. An officer of considerable distinction, to whom even his contemporary general officers deferred, Browning went from strength to strength after Sandhurst; he commanded the British Airborne Forces at Arnhem, became Comptroller to the Princess Elizabeth, and married that charming and accomplished writer, Daphne du Maurier.

But Uncle was not a Browning fan. To him, Boy Browning was just a Captain in the Grenadiers who gave him a lot of trouble at Sandhurst. The best he ever said about him was: 'Fuckin' GS bastard!' (Literally GS stands for General Service but it had become a synonym for all the unpleasant chores a soldier was burdened with in the Army.)

Years later, after the war, I returned to Sandhurst on an official visit. The year was 1949 and I was Commandant of the Pakistan Military Academy. Earlier that year, the RMC Sandhurst had been amalgamated with the RMA Woolwich and I was interested to see the changes that had occurred since my time.

On arrival I was met by the Assistant Adjutant, a major in the Irish Guards, who took me on a guided tour. When he mentioned that he had been in 5 Company as a cadet, I told him that I'd been in 'lovely Five' as well.

'Then you must have known Uncle,' he said.

Uncle, it seemed, had retired in 1948 after some thirty-five years at Sandhurst, and the Assistant Adjutant went on to tell me of the last encounter between Uncle and Boy Browning. The Major was not present himself, so the story may be apocryphal but it's a good one nonetheless and, knowing Uncle, it's more than likely true.

Shortly after the war, Browning had paid a return visit to Sandhurst, a lieutenant-general by now and covered in honours and awards. The Commandant asked him if there was anything special he wanted to see.

'Yes,' said Browning. 'Have you got any of the old servants here who might have been around in my day?'

So they checked and found two of the old and bold, Harry Groves and Uncle. The two servants were told to present themselves at the Commandant's office, still in their working clothes of shirt sleeves and green baize aprons. Harry went in first and endured the usual noncommittal conversation reserved for such occasions. Harry was a gentleman and knew all the correct responses. Not so Uncle. He stood outside the office door, chewing over all the imagined injuries of the past. Finally he was called in to see the great man.

'How are you, Uncle?' Browning asked. 'You look much the same.'

For a while Uncle said not a word; he sucked his teeth and fixed Browning with a baleful glare. Then he took a deep breath, leaned his hands on the table between them and, still staring into Browning's face, said: 'Jesuskerist, who'd'a thought they'd make you a fuckin' General!'

Well of course Browning laughed, and so I'm told did the Commandant. After all, Uncle had become an institution, and perhaps he was entitled to the last word.

16

3

Trooping to India

In 1929 I received my commission and left Sandhurst. It was sad, of course, saying goodbye to all one's friends, but my memories of that time are of enormous pride in my new status as a commissioned officer in His Majesty's Imperial Indian Army and wild excitement whenever I thought of what the future might bring.

Before I could sail out to India there were innumerable arrangements to be made. Chief among these was to acquire a whole new wardrobe for the hot climate, including new uniforms; because I was destined to join a cavalry regiment, ninety per cent of my RMC infantry-type uniform had to be discarded. My poor father was faced with yet another large bill. I took my old uniform to 'Ma' Hart who ran the hock shop in Camberley, not far from Sandhurst. It seemed a great waste to hand over hundreds of pounds' worth of beautiful clothes and receive only pennies in return but there was no alternative. What Ma did with the old uniforms no one knew, for incoming cadets would never be permitted to buy reach-me-down uniforms; perhaps she exported them to banana republics.

When I had done the rounds of all the tailors and outfitters I went out and bought a substantial wooden trunk, lined with tin, to store my clothing in when I reached India, particularly the woollens and serges. India is full of bugs of varying voracity: termites, moths and the insidious 'woolly bear', a minute furry insect that can ruin an unprotected drawerful of woollies in a single night. Cotton and drill garments, I was to find, were generally safe from predatory insects – but not from the *dhobi*, the Indian washerman. The *dhobi* plied his trade by a creek or river on the outskirts of every Indian cantonment (military station) or else in the long lines of concrete troughs provided by the municipality. He used the traditional method of washing, scrubbing the garments on a rock or concrete slab, whirling them round his head and crashing them down again; and the same treatment was meted out to every garment, no matter how delicate. One's bearer, or chief house servants, paid the *dhobi* a set monthly sum and for this he washed everything, regardless of quantity, including bed and table linen. As I was a bachelor my *dhobi* was paid about fifteen rupees a month, the 1929 equivalent of twenty-two shillings; a married couple would have paid slightly more, about twenty rupees.

My most precious piece of new equipment and the joy of my life was my brown leather 'Sam Browne' belt, which was made for me by Maxwells of Dover Street, the famous boot and shoe maker by appointment to His Majesty. This belt was invented by a British officer of Indian Cavalry, Samuel James Browne, who in 1849 raised in Lahore the 2nd Punjab Cavalry of the Punjab Frontier Force; later, in 1922, it was amalgamated with the 5th Punjab Cavalry and became the 12th Sam Browne's Cavalry (FF). Sam Browne was a gallant and distinguished officer. At Seerporah in the Indian Mutiny on 31 August 1858, Brevet-Major Sam Browne of the 2nd Cavalry, accompanied by a single trooper, charged and captured a rebel gun. He was severely wounded and lost his left arm, but he won that most coveted of decorations, the Victoria Cross. A couple of years later he was in action against the tribesmen of the North West Frontier and found considerable difficulty in carrying his sword when dismounted; so he designed a belt which would not only carry the sword comfortably when mounted or dismounted and leave the arms free, but which would also securely carry the pistol so that it didn't go off accidentally, as they so often did, and harm the wearer. The original belt is preserved in the Museum of the Royal Military College, Sandhurst. The use of the belt became almost universal. One wonders if Hitler's strutting storm troopers, or even the *flics* of Paris, had any idea that their cross-belts originated as the result of a minor skirmish on the plains of India over a hundred years ago.

Maxwells also made my polo and hunting boots, the former in soft brown leather and the latter in black. Polo boots were customarily worn when one was in uniform, and like everything else that Maxwells produced they were made of the finest leather, hand-stitched. As soon as I received them I made a special return trip to Sandhurst and sought out my old servant, Uncle; for a very modest fee, about a sovereign a pair, he returned them to me with an unbelievable finish and shine – the result of hours of elbow grease and the application of a bone of heelball and Kiwi dark tan.

I had been advised to buy a minimum of lightweight khaki drill uniforms in England, as the Indian drill lasted much longer; in any case, the cut and design of hot-weather uniforms often changed with the advent of a new CO in a particular regiment. The uniforms included caps and hats of all kinds, of course, and also the so-called 'Wolseley helmet', a topi or tropical sun hat. It was a hard hat, covered in khaki drill, with the brim bound in leather and a leather chinstrap that could either be worn under the chin or stowed atop the peak. Around the dome were several layers of carefully graded *pagri* cloth; in my regiment the topmost layer of cloth was blue with the regimental badge at the front. At the top of this elegant beehive was superimposed a sort of small cap that covered the ventilation hole. But I soon discovered the Wolseley helmet was both too thin and too heavy to make it an adequate sunshade. We kept them for ceremonial wear or for the cooler weather. In hot weather, when temperatures soared to over 100°F in the shade, we wore a thick lightweight sola topi which could only be bought in India.

Having collected my new wardrobe it was time to say goodbye to my family and friends. There were no lavish farewell parties at Invermark, however, as my mother was a chronic invalid and bedridden. In fact, she did not have long to live. To make her last days more tolerable my father had turned the drawing-room on the ground floor into a bedroom for her. There she was able to see at least part of her beautiful garden upon which she had lavished so much loving care. But the house was always full of nurses and companions and the hospital atmosphere did not lend itself to parties.

So my father took me out for a farewell lunch at my favourite London restaurant, the Hungaria near Piccadilly Circus, and my surviving brother Ivor treated me and a couple of lady friends to dinner and a night at the theatre, allowing me to choose which show to see. The play that I chose was *Journey's End*, a rather stark play about life in the trenches in the First World War – which may be indicative of my state of mind at the time. It was not the most cheerful of subjects but it was an excellent play and was enjoying great success in London at the time. The plot features shell-shock and the pressures which led to a young officer refusing to obey his company commander's orders to take part in a raid; the latter, reaching the end of his tether, confronts his shaky subordinate with a pistol and implies 'Either . . . Or . . .'. I had good reason to recall this plot some fifteen years later in Italy.

My final farewells completed, I caught a train from Waterloo to South-ampton. It was the first week of February, 1929. My orders were to report to the Embarkation Officer and then embark on His Majesty's Troopship *Nevasa*. A white, single-stack, coal-burning steamer, the *Nevasa* belonged to the British India Steamship Company but was on charter to the Government as a troopship. She was not a bad old tub, although possessed of few refinements and never at her best in heavy seas.

In effect, the ship was run by a complete field regiment of artillery (it was called a brigade in those days), though she was also carrying hundreds of drafted men who would be joining British infantry battalions or cavalry regiments stationed in India. She was full to the brim; between decks the hammocks swung and swayed like so many cocoons in a mulberry tree.

The day began with an hour of physical training for all hands. Later we were inspected by an endless gaggle of officers: the captain, the officer commanding troops, the troop officer (a ship's officer supercargo for this duty), the ship's adjutant, the field officer (a major or above) of the week, the ship's quartermaster (military), the duty officer of the day, the bosun and numerous matelots. Quite a procession. During their rounds we all had to stand to beside our hammocks or cots, if we weren't lying supine in helpless protest at the heaving seas.

One day as we were passing through the Bay of Biscay, notorious for its savage storms, I was appointed orderly officer of the day. The weather was appalling and the *Nevasa* was struggling to stay upright; she did everything but loop the loop. Nevertheless I was determined not to let the side down. I joined the rear of the prestigious 'crocodile' dressed in my best uniform, Sam Browne belt gleaming, and wearing my new Wolseley helmet; the latter seemed somewhat incongruous but such were the orders of the ship's adjutant. I was the very picture of a smart young officer going on duty for the first time.

At first all was well. I swayed and dipped to the roll of the ship as we passed through the upper decks, though by this time the storm was at its height. Then we descended a companionway and entered the troop decks. I had never seen such a shambles. Not a single man was standing to his hammock. All were stretched out on their backs or sides, retching and puking all over the decks and each other. The officers of the inspection line slipped and slithered as they processed down the lines of hammocks.

The stench lives with me still. I just couldn't stand it. The bile rose in my throat and I turned, thrusting my way through the lesser lights of the procession, heading for the nearest rail. After retching my heart out I staggered to my cabin and hoped for oblivion. It was not to be.

There was a bang on my cabin door. 'Ship's adjutant wants to see you, sir.'

I tidied myself as best I could and lurched along innumerable passageways to the Orderly Room. There I received the most imperial rocket for absenting myself without permission. I think I showed remarkable restraint; I should have thrown up on his immaculate desk. The brute was a sailing enthusiast and later became a major-general. I never liked him. They should have transferred him to the Navy. But years later I did have the satisfaction of beating his team in a polo tournament. He never knew why the opposing Number One rode him off the ball so savagely.

As we rounded the southern tip of Portugal, the weather improved and life aboard ship took on a pleasanter aspect. Apart from the daily inspection, the PT sessions, the mandatory boat and emergency drills, the routine left us plenty of time to ourselves. All of us young officers studied Urdu for an hour a day, the lingua franca of the Indian Army, receiving our instruction from young Indian cadets who were commissioned with us. We also whiled away long hours playing games or just lazing on the deck in the glorious sunshine. We officers played bridge, but the soldiers gathered on deck in large groups to play the only gambling game that was permitted: Housey-Housey. Today, under the less romantic-sounding name of Bingo, the game is played at both ends of the social scale, from church groups to international casinos. All day long their games went on with the callers shouting out 'clickety-click' (sixty-six), 'doctor's dilemma' (nine – referring, I believe, to the number of a potion alleged to be prescribed by medical officers when a patient's complaint could not be diagnosed), and 'top o' the 'ouse' (one hundred), hence the name of the game.

I had my first view of the famous Rock of Gibraltar, but we did not call in. We sailed along the North African coast and eventually put in at Malta, where some of the men were disembarked to join their parent units on the island. The rest of us were allowed a few hours ashore and I was enchanted by the place with its quaint old narrow streets and horse-drawn carriages. Sadly, many of these were demolished by saturation bombing in the war, all too evident when I returned to Malta in 1944, though the climate was still delightful and the people charming.

More lazy days were to follow before we entered the Suez Canal for a romantic passage through to the Red Sea. We also called in at Port Said and again were allowed ashore to explore the sights and sounds of our first eastern city. The chief attraction here was the cosmopolitan store on the waterfront, known world-wide as Simon Artz and full of goodies that an impecunious young subaltern could only admire and not buy: jewellery, Swiss watches, costly perfumes. The city itself was teeming with beggars, con men and pimps.

'You like my seester, sair? She just like Queen Victoria, got same tings you know, sair.'

'I get you a good diamind, sair – just like Kohinoor only cheaper.'

'You want to see donkey screw lady, sair? She verry famous lady, sair, from hareem of Sultan of Turkey, sair. She likum donkey verry much – you see, then p'raps you do later, no?'

But eventually we were back on ship, wallets and morals still intact.

The passage through the Red Sea seemed interminable; the days were blazing hot and the nights only slightly cooler. The *Nevasa* had no air-conditioning, of course, and sometimes the heat soared to about 120°F. I gained first-hand knowledge of the meaning of 'posh': Port Out, Starboard Home, posh people being able to afford the more expensive cabins on the side of the ship away from the sun. My cabin, shared with two other young men, was on the starboard side and the afternoon sun flooded in making anything metal impossible to touch. Canvas shoots were rigged in the shrouds to catch the little breezes that drifted by occasionally and channel them into the depths of the troop decks where soldiers lay sweating in their hammocks. Higher in the superstructure, the officers' cabins had metal scoops to fit in the portholes; these afforded some relief when the breeze came from dead ahead as the passage of the ship forced some air into the stifling cabins. The ship's crew rigged up a canvas 'swimming pool' on deck, about fifteen feet square and filled with seawater, but it is dubious whether the water in the pool was any cooler than the air outside. The only way to get a fair night's sleep was to hump a mattress and pillows up on to the deck, though one had to be quick to wake up or one's slumbers were terminated by a sluice of seawater from a firehose, as the crew had to swab down the decks before sunrise.

Our next port of call was Aden, sometimes called 'the Crossroads of the Empire', where the *Nevasa* had to replenish her bunkers. As we dropped anchor, from all directions there appeared tugs and lighters filled with coal from the mines of South Wales. Walkways were erected from barge to ship and hundreds of near-naked coolies swarmed aboard, swaying under the baskets of dusty coal they carried on their heads. All day long the ship was enveloped in clouds of coal dust, which got into everything – clothing, bedding, food, and even into the drinking-water supplies. Some of us fled ashore for an hour or two, though there was little to do; the town and hinterland certainly lived up to that famous piper's tune 'The Barren Rocks of Aden'. We retreated to the Officers' Club, which had a small swimming beach, safely cut off from the Indian Ocean by a steel fence to keep out the sharks. I have never had any desire to return to Aden.

Once the ship left the heated land and sailed out into the ocean, our lives became more comfortable. It was still hot but the days and nights were livened by sea breezes. About two days out from Aden, however, we were to learn what happens when there is an emergency at sea.

It was a tradition aboard ship to hold a fancy-dress ball towards the end of the voyage. There were not many ladies on board the *Nevasa*: a few officers' wives, a daughter or two and about five nursing sisters, members of Queen Alexandra's Imperial Nursing Service who staffed the military hospitals throughout the Empire. They wore no badges of rank, indeed in those days they were not entitled to a rank; they were officially addressed as 'Sister' until they were appointed 'Matron'. But matrons were a power in the Army; even generals deferred to them.

Once, while I was still a cadet at Sandhurst, I had suffered a badly broken collar bone and was admitted to the big Cambridge Hospital in Aldershot. It was here that I encountered 'Tiger Mac', a Scottish lady with a name like Mackenzie or Macmullan or something. She was a very senior matron and ruled the Cambridge with a rod of iron; even colonels who became her patients practically called her 'sir'. In Tiger Mac's presence, all was order and calm. But when the coast was clear, another cadet and I used to fool around with a very attractive young sister called Ailsa McPhail. One evening I happened to have my hands on a soda-water siphon when Ailsa walked into the ward. She was in full uniform of grey dress, short red-lined cape falling to the waist and starched white cap down to the shoulders. Standing there in the doorway she presented an irresistible target. I pressed the siphon and let out a well aimed stream. But Ailsa ducked, just as Tiger Mac walked through the door behind her, smack into the jet of water. She let out a roar that a drill sergeant would have been proud of and ordered us back to bed; Ailsa was banished from the officers' ward and the following day I was discharged prematurely. On my return to Sandhurst the company commander sent for me and, after giving me a mild rocket, offered me some sage advice: not to fool around with nursing sisters while they were on duty, and above all to steer clear of the Tiger Macs of this world.

But on board the *Nevasa* the nursing sisters were not on duty, and they were much in demand at the fancy-dress ball. The ball was for first-class passengers only; the soldiery did not get this type of entertainment. Even so, the lack of female partners meant that most of us had to go without, so it developed into a real bash. On such occasions the senior officers tended to wink at the surfeit of booze, provided the inebriates behaved in a reasonably gentlemanly manner. A good time was had by all, and most of us staggered back to our cabins in the early hours of the next morning. I had just fallen into a sodden stupor when the alarm bells sounded all around the ship.

Clutching my old-fashioned cork lifejacket I made my way to my lifeboat station along with all the other sheep. There was no obvious sign of an emergency; the ship was stopped but seemed to be on an even keel. Then the order came down: 'Call the roll! Man overboard!'

Slowly the vessel turned around and steamed back over her course, searchlights scanning the dark sea. Befuddled heads asked each other what had happened, who was missing. Gradually we pieced the story together. The missing man was 'Rookie' Thunder. It seemed that one of his companions, as drunk as the rest of us, had noticed Rookie's bunk was vacant; a short wait convinced him that Rookie was not attending a call of nature, so he oozed into the passageway shouting at the top of his voice, '*Man overboard!*' An equally inebriated staff officer bumped into him and, failing to question his assumption, joined in the chorus: 'Man overboard!' Before long, everyone believed that Rookie had gone to Davy Jones's locker. A search of the ship seemed to confirm the fact.

The *Nevasa*'s officers were obliged to follow the required procedure; they turned the ship around and searched the ocean for hours, making out the usual reports, all without success. There was no sign of Rookie.

By dawn the ship had resumed her course for Bombay. Naturally none of us had gone back to bed; we stood around in small groups discussing the situation and debating what we would do if we fell overboard. We all agreed that the chance of rescue was one in a thousand. Some said they'd take a deep breath and go under; others said they'd never give up, but would swim until exhausted. With the callousness of youth, I don't think any of us were unduly upset.

Suddenly there was a shout and someone was pointing down at the foredeck. We all surged forward, staring down at one of the forward lifeboats. From beneath the boat covers a figure had emerged. It climbed down out of the boat and stood on the deck, stretching out both arms in the full rays of the rising sun. The man was stark bollock naked. It was Rookie.

The officer of the watch had spotted him too. Whistles were blown and there was a moment's bustle as two burly quartermasters were despatched to grab the culprit. Rookie was quite unperturbed by all the fuss; indeed, he displayed great sang-froid as he was marched off, still naked, for lengthy questioning. He had no idea how he came to be in the lifeboat, he said, nor how he had lost his clothes. Later that day he was placed under 'open arrest', remanded for trial by the Sub Area Commander, Bombay. I heard later that he was let off with a reprimand, but he had certainly found a novel way to join His Majesty's Imperial Indian Army.

A few days later HMT *Nevasa* docked at Bombay. It was my first sight of India, but such was the confusion that my initial impressions were swamped in a swirl of movement, dust and heat.

For some obscure reason, those of us who were joining the Indian Army were not immediately permitted to join the regiments for which we were destined. Our names appeared on a back page of the Army List under the heading 'Unattached List for the Indian Army'. This was a typical British mis-statement, however, for we had all been 'attached', albeit temporarily, to a British infantry battalion on the Indian Establishment. In my case I found myself assigned to the 2nd Battalion, the Essex Regiment – the Pompadours, as they were known, from the pompadour purple that was their regimental colour. As a result, we all faced a year on temporary attachment, going over the same routine as at Sandhurst: foot drill, King's Regulations, the Manual of Military Law, etc. We were allowed to command a platoon of British soldiers, but not the Indians we had come to India to serve with. Still, it was all good experience, as I was to find out.

Within a couple of days of disembarking I had been given my rail passes to join the Pompadours, then stationed the farthest north of any British battalion: at Landi Kotal in the Khyber Pass, facing Afghanistan. So, one spring-like day in March, 1929, I caught the Frontier Mail from Bombay to Peshawar.

4

Frontier Mail

The distance between Bombay and Peshawar is over thirteen hundred miles, and in 1929 the train journey took about three days and two nights to complete. It was a fascinating journey, though, and a wonderful way to see the country for the first time.

There were two main rail routes between Bombay and Delhi, the capital: one route, via Rutlam, was run by the Great Indian Peninsular (GIP) Railway; the other, via Baroda, by the Bombay, Baroda and Central Indian (BB & CI) Railway. From Delhi on to Peshawar it was the same train. On the Frontier Mail – all the trains had similar splendid names – I took the BB & CI route, along with three others of my group who were to be dropped off at different places en route; I was the only one going the whole way to Peshawar. We shared a four-berth compartment in a first-class carriage.

Indian trains of that era were drawn by huge locomotives, either coal- or wood-burning. Generally main-line trains were twelve or fourteen coaches long, with the third-class coaches immediately behind the engine, second-class behind them and the first-class coaches and restaurant car at the rear. The closer the engine the more the passengers suffered from smoke, smuts and cinders. And those old locomotives did spew cinders: one would find them in the bedding, the food, even in the drinking water.

The bulk of travellers used the third-class, which had no bunks, just rows of hard benches packed with humanity. Sometimes the overflow was such that people spilled out of the windows and stood on the running board or perched precariously on the roof of the lurching carriages. Whenever the train pulled in at a station there was always a frantic surge as people pushed forward, trying to enter the third-class coaches. Not that everyone paid; the Indian Railways did have ticket inspectors but in the scrum their job was well nigh impossible.

Second-class accommodation, chiefly patronized by middle-class Indians and Anglo-Indians, was a more spartan version of first-class, which consisted of two-berth and four-berth compartments with a separate compartment for the personal servants of first-class passengers. The *sahib log* (basically white people) and the more affluent Indians travelled first-class. However, no matter how affluent, an Indian would never dream of sharing a compartment already occupied by a sahib if he could possibly avoid it. Certain young Britishers were often very rude to anyone they considered a 'wog' (Westernized Oriental Gentleman), a term of opprobrium that was only too well understood by Indians. I think it was Evelyn Waugh who coined the phrase 'The wogs begin at Calais', and I regret to say that there were many Englishmen abroad who lived according to this tenet. This was true even of some who had been at Sandhurst, where we lived alongside Indian cadets and it had been obvious to even the most insular intelligence that, given a difference in race and certain religious taboos (generally in connection with food and the preparation thereof), they lived by the same standards and were just as much 'gentlemen' as we were. On the other hand, there were also certain orthodox Indians, particularly of the Hindu faith, who would consider themselves defiled if they lived even for an hour or two in the company of an unbeliever.

Our four-berther on the Frontier Mail consisted of two lower and two upper bunks; by day the latter were hooked up to the roof and we all sat on the lower bunks. Each compartment had its own small bathroom with a tiny handbasin and a shower stall, both fed from a steel tank located on the roof. The water temperature depended on the air temperature outside: in summer it was scalding hot, in winter it was icy, and there was no way of regulating the system. The toilet consisted of an open vent directly above the permanent way, ('No, darling, you'll have to wait. You simply can't do it while we're standing in the station!')

In the 1920s there were no air-conditioned coaches on the trains. Two small electric fans churned the turgid air overhead but we didn't even have the benefit of the refinement that was introduced in the '30s. This was a large block of ice which one could order before starting one's journey; it was placed in a container on the floor of the compartment and the fans were directed on to it to circulate cooler air. The ice blocks weighed eighty to a hundred pounds apiece but in the extreme heat they lasted only a few hours.

The carriage doors were heavy and could be locked from the inside. Three glazed windows on either side of the compartment were each covered with a framed wire gauze and a sliding wooden shutter. Theoretically all could be bolted shut but in fact they were very insecure; a smart bang on the outside caused the shutter, gauze and window each in turn to fall into its slot, enabling an intruder to enter the compartment. This was by no means uncommon, particularly at night when the occupants were asleep. Any noise the intruder made was covered by the constant rattle and clatter of the train. Professional thieves would wait in the darkness on station platforms and leap onto the running board as the train passed slowly through. As cunning as they were agile, they would stand on the running board until they were sure the occupants of a compartment were asleep, then open a window and quest with one hand for watch, wallet or handbag. Having made a haul they either climbed on to the roof or rode the buffers until the train slowed down at the next station when they would jump off and disappear into the night.

Most of them were petty thieves and comparatively harmless, but sometimes the trains were worked by real thugs, armed and prepared to do murder if necessary. In fact, one of my fellow cadets from Sandhurst was to lose his life in just such an incident.

At Sandhurst George Hext had acquired an unusual nickname. It was given to him on our very first parade when Sergeant-Major Manger was proceeding down the ranks, teaching us all to give our names in the correct manner. He halted in front of George and cast a sardonic glance at the monocle that George always wore in his right eye.

'And what's your name, sir?'

'Hext, Staff.'

'Ho, Mr Hext, sir, and what may I arsk is that in your right eye?'

'It's a monocle, Staff.'

'Well, Mr Hext, sir, you'd only need one in the hother end and you'd be a bloody telescope, wouldn't you, sir?'

And so George Hext was known thereafter as 'the bloody telescope'.

Anyway, George came to India with the rest of us and, like me, joined a battalion in northern India. One day, two or three years later, he and another subaltern by the name of Saunders were travelling south to attend a course in Central India. The two men were sharing a compartment on the Frontier Mail, along with George's dog, a bull terrier. It was their first night on the train, somewhere in the Punjab near Ambala. As usual, before going to sleep they locked and barred all doors and windows; but in the middle of the night a gang of thugs burst into the compartment, waking George and his companion.

Although unarmed, the two officers put up a spirited resistance and a fierce hand-to-hand fight ensued. But the thugs had knives. Saunders received serious wounds, George and his dog were stabbed to death.

Saunders managed to pull the communication cord to slow the train, but it was too late: the thugs had fled.

There is a sad sequel to this story. When Saunders's wounds were treated he insisted on proceeding to his destination though he swore that never again would he travel unarmed. He duly completed the course and before setting off on the return journey he acquired a .45 pistol. This time he travelled alone. Not far from the place where Saunders had been attacked on his way south, the train made an unscheduled stop. Just as the train was pulling out of the small station, there was a sudden crash and the window shutter fell down. The head and shoulders of a man were silhouetted against the receding lights. Saunders took aim and fired, the figure disappeared, and once again Saunders pulled the communication cord. It turned out that he had shot and killed the teenage son of the local Anglo-Indian station master.

At the court of enquiry it was revealed that the lad always 'jumped' trains in this way; brought up in the railways he never bought a ticket. As usual he had stepped up onto the running board and banged on the nearest window. He would have asked permission to enter, but on this occasion he was denied the chance.

Saunders finally faced a court martial on a charge of manslaughter. I was told that he was so shattered by these two tragedies that, at the age of twenty-three, his hair turned white almost overnight.

Fortunately, no such incident occurred on this train journey. To pass the time, my three companions and I played endless games of bridge, vingt-et-un and piquet, in between watching the countryside pass and speculating on our future. And, every four hours or so, we were able to disembark when the train stopped at a major station. We would climb out onto the platform and wend our way, through hundreds of milling peasants trying to board the train, towards the restaurant car at the rear.

There is something very appealing to me about dining aboard a train, even if the food is not of the best. In fact, the food served on Indian trains was really quite good: chiefly curry, of course, but we were new to the country and it seemed only right and proper that our initial culinary experiences should include this traditional dish. The meals tended to be long and leisurely as we could not return to our compartment until the train stopped at the next station. The waiter brought us round after round of *chota* pegs – literally a small peg (shot) of scotch, usually with ice and soda; this was the customary tipple of the *sahib log* in India.

And still the countryside slipped past. At first it all seemed the same, mile after mile of flat dusty brown plains with the occasional small hillock. By night the scene was dotted with endless tiny fires as families prepared their evening meal. I can still smell the aroma of burning cow dung to this day; it is strangely pleasant, quite unlike any other smell I have encountered. During the day we could see dozens of these cow dung patties drying out for use on the fire, either on the ground or on the walls of the mud huts. Decent sized trees are practically nonexistent over much of India, so dried cow dung is the only available fuel. Sometimes a new and enthusiastic civil servant would try to persuade the peasants to spread the dung on their fields, to improve the poor quality of the soil. But their attempts were in vain; cow dung was too precious as a fuel to be wasted like that.

Gradually, as the train headed ever north, the character of the countryside began to change and I saw more and more green fields where sugar cane, mustard and other crops were grown. This was the first sign that I was approaching the Punjab, for the fields were irrigated by man-made channels deriving their source from the great Punjabi rivers. The very name Punjab means 'Land of the Five Rivers': *panch* (five) and *ab* (water).

By the time we reached Rawalpindi I was alone in the compartment, my three friends having left the train at earlier stops. I gazed out of the windows more eagerly now, aware that I should later come to know this country on the most intimate terms, and as the train drew into the terminal at Peshawar Cantonment my excitement grew. This was the Frontier, land of the Khyber Pass, through which all the great invasions of India had come – Alexander the Great and the Moguls, to name but two.

Slowly the train came to a halt against the buffers, and waiting for me on the platform was Wahidullah Khan.

5

Peshawar to Landi Kotal

Wahidullah was to be my first bearer or personal servant. He was a Pathan; his English was halting and I knew little Urdu but he managed to explain that I should go with him. I was to stay in a hotel in Peshawar until the following day, when a party from the Essex Regiment would be coming down the Khyber, and I could go back with them.

It seemed strange to me that there was no official communication from the battalion to which I had been attached; but I thought what the hell, this is India, things are obviously different here. Back in Bombay I had sent a telegram to the battalion, in accordance with what I'd learnt of service customs and etiquette while at Sandhurst, indicating my expected time of arrival at the station in Peshawar. But I might have known: no one was particularly interested in the arrival of another attached officer – no one, that is, save Wahidullah.

In fact it was pure chance that led Wahidullah to meet me. He had got the buzz from one of the battalion's mess servants, who overheard the Adjutant mention my expected arrival to the CO at breakfast. Wahidullah was without a job; he decided to appoint himself my bearer. He collected his 'chits' (references from previous masters) and caught the next bus to Peshawar.

Wahidullah took control of all my gear, tipped the coolies (porters) and hailed two *tongas*, one for himself and one for me. The *tonga* was the most common form of public hire vehicle in those days when taxis were so few and far between; it was a two-wheeled trap, usually drawn by an emaciated pony, with the driver sitting up front and the passenger behind him, facing backwards. My luggage was piled up around me and off we set for Dean's Hotel.

Dean's was the only European-style hotel in Peshawar, well known before I was born. Officers usually stayed at the Officers' Club but of course I was not yet a member. It was my first introduction to an up-country hotel and I founded it clean and quite comfortable. My accommodation consisted of a bed/sitting-room with a bathroom leading off it. The principal piece of furniture was a *charpoy*, a wooden-framed bed strung with broad bands of cotton tape; above the bed a mosquito net was supported by light bamboo poles. One had to supply one's own bedding – every sahib travelled with a canvas holdall containing mattresses, sheets, blanket and pillow. To complete the furniture there was a plain wooden writing desk with an upright chair and a lounging chair made of cane with long extensions upon which to stretch one's legs. A large electric fan hung overhead.

The bathroom was equally basic: an enamel washbasin and jug reposing on a wooden stand and a large galvanized tin washtub stood on the brick floor. Beside the tub was a big earthenware pot called a *chatti* containing cold water. When one wanted to bathe, one's bearer sent for the *bhisti*, the water-carrier, as all who have read Kipling's *Gunga Din* will know. The *bhisti* kept a number of five-gallon kerosene drums heating on an open fire and when called he would dump ten gallons of boiling water into the tub, then add cold water from the *chatti*. As for that final necessity, the bathroom contained an enamel chamber pot – the 'peespa' as the bearer called it – and also a 'thunder box', a wooden commode holding an enamel receptacle with a lid. These two pots were removed for emptying and cleaning by the sweeper, a low-caste person, for none of the other servants would do such dirty work; he dumped the contents into a large can which was itself emptied after dark into a wheeled canister drawn by a bullock and driven by another sweeper. Such was the crude but universal system throughout up-country India.

The following day the party duly arrived from the Essex Regiment: a subaltern named 2nd Lt Hazelton, a couple of NCOs and twenty men. But they had come to Peshawar not to escort me to my new battalion at Landi Kotal, but to collect the battalion's pay for the month.

First the men were given a couple of days off, though there was nothing much for them to do other than meet the men of another British battalion, the King's Own Yorkshire Light Infantry, stationed in Peshawar. Hazelton booked into the Officers Club; I stayed on at Dean's but naturally I spent the days with him, eager to hear about Landi Kotal and the battalion to which I was now attached.

As soon as their short break was over, Hazelton and his men went to the

Imperial Bank of India in Peshawar and I went with them. I was astonished to find that, according to regulations, we had to count the money ourselves, a very long and laborious procedure. Not only did we have to count each individual note, already counted out into bundles by the bank's staff, but we also had to open every single roll of coins, count them and stuff them back into the original packets; then Hazelton had to certify that every last coin and note had been checked. At that time the Imperial Bank of India was not a commercial bank but a part of the machinery of government, and it struck me as odd that the certification of a very junior officer should carry more weight than the head cashier of a government bank.

Eventually the money was counted. It was loaded into a large cast-iron cash box, the lid was shut and secured with a massive padlock, and the whole box was wrapped with a huge chain with links as big as a man's index finger. Then the box was heaved onto a *tonga* for transport to the railway station – the poor pony could barely stagger forward under its weight – with the escort marching alongside.

For the final part of my rail journey from Peshawar to Landi Kotal I discovered that I would be travelling in a second-class carriage, along with the soldiers and the cash box. We were all herded into the train and the box was secured to the compartment floor, the chain being passed through iron rings let into the floor. This was the regular procedure; every local knew that this was how the battalion's cash was transported. Even if the local tribesmen raided the train and overran the very small escort, their efforts would meet with doubtful rewards for they would have to destroy the coach to get at the box.

Our train consisted of only a few coaches, but even so we had two locomotives at the front and two more at the rear, to pull and push us up the steep sides of the Khyber Pass. As a romantically inclined newcomer to this famous outpost of Empire, I was impatient to get going, but to Hazelton and the others this was just part of their routine. At last the train pulled out of Peshawar, heading for the ever-turbulent Frontier. This was where the young soldier could learn his business of fighting a real enemy – and perhaps win his spurs.

The Frontier, as opposed to the North West Frontier Province of which Peshawar was the capital, was a strip of land some fifty to a hundred miles wide between British India and Afghanistan. Nowhere was there a clear demarcation except at road crossing places such as Landi Khana, only a few miles beyond Landi Kotal where I was destined to live.

Part settled and part unsettled, the Frontier was inhabited by various warrior tribes: Afridi, Mahsud, Shinwari and others. All are fair-skinned, many are blue-eyed; it is said they are descended from Alexander's phalanxes. Generically they are Pathans and speak a language of their own called Pashto; in some areas the language is soft, in others harsh and guttural, but it is the same from north to south.

In those days the tribal areas were defined within a theoretical boundary known as the Durand Line, an arbitrary line drawn on a map in 1893 by a civil servant of that name in the Government of India. But the Frontier was always in turmoil and many of the Frontier towns had quite large garrisons of the regular army to protect local settlers as well as to police the border. There were also some garrisons stationed inside tribal territory, the largest being at Razmak, and the road connecting Razmak with the outside world was picketed with troops to project those escorting the convoys of supplies. Like many a remote garrison, Razmak was plagued by tribal raiders; armed and belligerent, the tribesmen were a constant threat. Even among themselves, any disagreement was customarily settled in blood and blood feuds were carried on from generation to generation.

In addition to the regular army garrisons, some tribal areas were semi-controlled by groups of irregulars recruited from among the tribesmen, generally called Levies or Scouts; this served not only to relieve the pressure on the regular army but also to keep at least some of the tribesmen out of trouble. Their officers were British, seconded from the regular army, and their corps were famous: the South Waziristan Scouts, the Kurrum Militia, the Zhob Militia and the Gilgit Scouts, to name just a few. Many British officers, once bitten with this type of service, stayed for ever, sacrificing advancement in their own regiments.

Britishers were not permitted to move about in tribal territory, unless in a formal convoy or with an escort of *khassadars* – 'insurance men' as I called them. They were hired from the local villages, recruited and paid by the Political Officer who lived in the fort located within the Landi Kotal camp; he also provided them with a uniform of sorts, a khaki shirt and trousers, and some .303 ammunition. The *khassadars* all had their own rifles, either stolen or copies of the Army's .303 SMLE (Short Muzzle Lee-Enfield); to them the ammunition – the real stuff, as opposed to the doubtful home-made variety – was worth more than gold. And they were effective. Had any British officer been killed while under their care, not only would official retribution follow swiftly but the *khassadar* system would be stopped, drawing down the ire of the tribal chiefs; the miscreants would probably be killed in their turn by their own people, for 'spoiling the market'. I was to spend many days escorted by these men, wandering over this grand country on the borders with Afghanistan.

As our train puffed and pulled its way up into the Khyber Pass I became ever more fascinated by the wild mountainous scenery and eagerly hopped

34

out at each station, along with the riflemen posted on either side of the coach.

The overall impression was of a rocky barren country dotted with tribal villages and the occasional military post or fort. All the villages were walled in, each with a watchtower standing over it; not even the locals moved about at night unless on some nefarious foray. There were small patches of cultivation surrounding each village, but the soil was poor and their attempts at agriculture looked pretty ineffectual to me. Indeed, as I later learned, were it not for the annual subsidy the villagers received from the government – in return for good behaviour – and the rake-off they got from camel caravans travelling through the Pass, they would have been penniless and forced to pursue a life of banditry. At the India end of the Pass was the ominous-looking fort of Jamrud. Standing like a huge brown battleship, its walls and bastions over ten feet thick, it guarded the entrance to the Pass as well as being a checkpoint for the endless *kafilas* (caravans) that daily crossed the border with Afghanistan. Three routes run through the Pass: the caravan road, the motor road and the railway. The caravans follow the stream bed, motor vehicles the easier contours, and the railway zigzags its way along the cliffsides through dozens of tunnels. The railway climbs over two thousand feet in twenty miles, often up gradients of 1 in 33. When it was built, for strategic reasons, in 1920–25 it was considered an impossible undertaking and on completion it excited the admiration of railway engineers all over the world.

The first twelve miles of the Pass are particularly impressive as the railway runs through Ali Masjid gorge, between narrow clefts and towering cliffs dominated by the peak of Tartarra, rising sheer to 6800 feet. Here one can see how impregnable the Pass must have seemed to ancient invaders. After the gorge the Pass widens out considerably, in some places to a mile or two, and there are more villages and signs of cultivation.

At last we reached Landi Kotal, the military cantonment where I would spend the next few months on attachment to the Essex Regiment.

Apart from the military cantonment, Landi Kotal comprised a fort, a *caravanserai* or inn to accommodate travellers with the camel trains, and of course the railway station. The cantonment housed two infantry battalions, one British and one Indian, as well as a mountain battery, a brigade HQ and several ancillary units including a joint (British and Indian) hospital. The third battalion of the brigade, usually Gurkhas, held the frontier post five miles away at Landi Khana, on the Frontier with Afghanistan.

In my day the camp was not a very aesthetic picture, but it was compact: row upon row of neatly spaced mud-walled barracks with corrugated iron roofs. As Landi Kotal stands on a high plateau the winters here were bitterly cold and these corrugated iron roofs provided very little insulation from the weather, allowing the cold to penetrate in winter and acting as a griddle during the searing heat of summer. The camp was enclosed within a triple barbed-wire apron with defensive posts sited at tactical intervals and gates that were normally kept locked. Outside the gates was the area of the fort and just beyond the perimeter to the east lay an emergency landing ground. The gates were manned by day and all local people needed a valid pass to enter, but at night the various posts were also manned, with searchlights playing upon the terrain outside the barbed wire. Anyone approaching the camp was challenged and if he didn't respond he would be fired upon. The fort itself was small and out of date; it played no part in the cantonment's defences.

The *caravanserai* was fascinating, an endless scene of movement and colour. The traders and travellers came from all over Central Asia and the bulk of their goods was carried on camels, ponies and donkeys. On any given day one might hear a dozen different languages and dialects being spoken. I spent many interesting hours in the *serai* – escorted, of course, by two or more *khassadars* to ensure the sightseer's safety. Few of the traders bothered to open their bales at Landi Kotal, preferring to keep their wares for sale at the big city markets of Peshawar and Delhi; but I did manage to make one precious buy. This was an Isfahan carpet, depicting the Tree of Life in the most luscious colours with all the animals looking very lifelike. I have the carpet to this day and have been told by experts that these Tree of Life carpets were usually made in pairs; so I suspect that the one I have was stolen – particularly as the dealer was so eager to sell.

As for the Essex Regiment itself, I found it efficient but typically dull. As in many British infantry battalions at that time, the officers were enmeshed in a stultifying promotion block. Many of the subalterns had more than twenty years' service behind them, but still were only responsible for platoons of thirty men and had no prospect of getting command of a company for years to come. The Colonel himself, a rather pompous man and lacking in any sense of humour, wasn't going any further after his tenure of command. My company commander, Captain Grimwood, had had an excellent career during the First World War when he won the DSO and attained the rank of full colonel; later he was sent with a detachment aboard a British cruiser to Danzig, to install the great Polish pianist Paderewski as the first premier of an independent Poland. But now Grimwood was way down the list of captains in the regular army, though at least he had his own company.

The men were a good lot, mostly from London and the eastern counties, but they led a very dull life. The majority had signed on for seven years with the colours and five years with the reserve. This meant that if a man who enlisted in England had been posted to a battalion just about to start its tour of foreign service, he might spend all of his seven years overseas – a dim prospect in places like Landi Kotal. They were poorly paid, something over a shilling a day, but the only place they could spend it was in the 'wet canteen' on beer, eggs and potatoes or in a poorly stocked Indian bazaar selling cheap brass pieces and the like. Amusement was limited to sport or the occasional film show in the so-called cinema, featuring old silent movies accompanied by someone playing a rinkidink piano. The terrain was too rocky for football, so the main game was field hockey at which the men excelled. The only other entertainment was a twice-yearly concert party, with lots of talent and generally a topical rollicking show.

On the whole I got on well with the men of Eleven Platoon. They were an ordinary bunch, none of them outstanding soldiers, but good dependable footsloggers who would fight doggedly when called upon, and I learned a lot from them – above all, how to deal with miscreants. The key, I found, was to be fair but firm. Each man had a crime sheet, or 'sheet roll' as it was called, which followed him throughout his service; but most crimes were of such a trivial nature that it struck me as unfair to enter them for ever on the records. A sharp 'dressing down' was enough to meet the needs of most situations; I made it plain that I was not to be fooled with and the men clearly respected this.

In Eleven Platoon there was one man who had a whole book of minor crimes: Private Connolly. When he joined the Army he had been asked if he had any 'previous trade or profession' and he had answered 'burglary'; at the top of his sheet, therefore, was the one word 'Burglar'. This was followed by scores of minor misdemeanours committed throughout his career. But the first time he came before me, I told him that his sheet roll was full enough already without me adding to it and that he and I were going to have a new and better relationship. And we did.

Private Worts was more of a problem. He was continually scrapping with his comrades and all because of his name. Otherwise a rather insignificant character, he could be roused to a fury by anyone calling him 'Warts'; he insisted that his name should be pronounced 'Werts'. Naturally the others enjoyed baiting him, until he resorted to fisticuffs and thus ended up with a formal rebuke from me.

Another problem character in my platoon was Private Carter who had family trouble at home in England; long before I joined he had started applying for compassionate transfer but all his requests had been denied. About this time a man from another company was invalided home to the UK as a mental case, genuinely and seriously ill. It seemed that Carter had been studying him and decided that he too would go 'mental'. He stopped talking to anyone and started doing odd things like sleepwalking around the barrack square in the early hours of the morning. The day came when he felt he had built up a sufficient dossier of strange behaviour and he reported sick. Now in a British battalion, a 'sick parade' is just that, a parade: the sick are marched to hospital and stand to attention when being questioned by the doctor. No CO likes a long sick roll; it reflects badly on the discipline of the battalion, so any man given 'M & D' (Medicine and Duty) usually ends up being treated as a company defaulter. But this was no deterrent to Private Carter. He told the orderly sergeant simply that he had 'a pain' and was marched off to the military hospital.

The hospital was commanded by a charming but tough Irishman, Major Power. He asked Carter what was wrong with him, and listened with growing interest to a moving story of stomach pains, early morning sickness and a swollen belly.

'I'm pregnant, that's what I am, sir, I'm pregnant!' Carter ended triumphantly. 'An' I can prove it too, sir. I got 'ere a list o' the prospective fathers – Colonel Bowen, Captain Prowse, the Adjutant and . . .'

Needless to say, Carter ended up on a charge and one more crime was added to his military case sheet. But I had a word with Captain Grimwood and we managed to have Carter transferred to another battalion, one that was due for posting to the UK in the near future. I can only hope that once he was home Carter was able to settle his family trouble.

Like everyone else, I found that life at Landi Kotal soon began to pall. Our duties were never very onerous and I longed with youthful eagerness for my year on attachment to be over, yearning to join the Bengal Lancers and perhaps see some real action. Fortunately, towards the end of the summer, the battalion was transferred to a much more civilized place, Nowshera, only a few miles from Peshawar.

Nowshera was hardly a centre of social activity but at least we were no longer cooped up inside barbed wire all day and night. There was a cricket club, a golf course and even English ladies to keep us amused. I began to enjoy life again. But before I left to join my own Regiment, I was to fall foul of the CO.

For a while I could do no wrong in the CO's eyes. He discovered that I was good at map reading, so he made me the battalion's Intelligence Officer and gave me a pony to carry out my duties. He also approved of my cricketing prowess for I had made a fair number of runs for the battalion cricket team and we had reached the final of the Northern Cricket Championship. It was about three weeks before I was due to leave and I knew the CO had already submitted his report about me to my future commanding officer; I also knew that this report was good.

Then it happened: the sergeants' mess ball, which fell on a Saturday, the eve of the championship final. Along with some other junior officers I had been invited to attend this ball, given by a British cavalry regiment stationed some fourteen miles away. Little did I know it then, but there was a tradition at sergeants' dances to waylay young officers from another unit and make them drunk. The favoured method involved 'heel-taps', when the victim's glass would be surreptitiously filled and refilled with all kinds of mixed drinks. I was only twenty years of age and I knew precious little about hard liquor – or the world itself, come to that. My father had brought me up to enjoy good wine and to drink whisky in moderation, but in fact I couldn't afford to drink much anyway.

Needless to say I became one of the victims that night. Well after midnight I was poured into someone's car and decanted at my quarters. I felt no pain. But at 5 am the next morning I was retching my heart out. I had never experienced anything like it before, nor have I experienced anything like it since. I was *sick*. My bearer, knowing that I was due on battalion church parade at 9 am, sent for my friends and together they did what they could with ice packs, aspirin, cold tea, black coffee. But I was still vomiting. The world seemed upside down. How I made it on parade I shall never know, but my sword was shaking like a feather in my right hand. There then followed the six-mile march to church, and back again after the service. Returning to my quarters I was still drunk when I fell into bed. Again my faithful bearer sent for the relief squad – who reminded me that the cricket final was due to start at 1.30 pm, and poured more tea, coffee and aspirin down my throat. At last I was on my feet; my vision was blurred and I felt awful, but apparently I looked compos mentis.

It was about 4.30 pm when I wobbled on to the cricket ground on my bicycle. My team was batting, eight men were already out and two men were at the wickets. There was only me left. Then, as I was strapping on my pads and selecting a bat, another batsman was out. But the team needed only five more runs to win – a mere bagatelle. I strolled to the crease and prepared to receive the first ball.

Before the first delivery, however, the wicket keeper ambled past me down the pitch and had a word with the bowler; I realized later that he must have seen my shaky hand and smelt my breath. At the time I only realized that the man I faced had a reputation as a fast bowler. I wound myself up in readiness.

The bowler grinned, walked slowly up to deliver, and tossed the ball gently at me: a simple shot, what children call 'a lollipop'. I swung my bat frantically – and missed. The ball had knocked my wicket down. I was out. My team had lost.

I don't think I have ever felt so ashamed. I deserved an imperial blast, and got it. The CO called me every despicable name he could think of, right there in front of the two assembled teams. He said that if it were possible he would retrieve the report on me and tear it up. Fortunately, he couldn't. Three weeks later I was on my way to join my own Regiment, reputation unsullied but with a very useful lesson learned. I have basically stuck to scotch and soda ever since.

6

Frontier Policy in Mobilization

It was 1930 and the 6th Lancers were stationed at a place called Sialkot, not far from Lahore. I quickly settled in, eager to learn my business and relishing my position as a young officer in the cavalry. Best of all, I discovered that it was likely I would see some real action at last, for even before I joined the Regiment I had begun to grasp the fact that trouble was brewing in northern India.

When British regiments first went to India in the days of the East India Company, there were 'King's Regiments' and 'Company Regiments'. At first they were wholly British; later the East India Company enlisted Indians, under British officers. The latter were often gentlemen adventurers who went out to India with the hope of making a quick fortune in a country continuously at war. The fruits of victory went to the winner and many a younger son returned to England with well-lined pockets. After the sepoys (Indian soldiers) mutinied in 1857, all units in India were removed from the jurisdiction of the East India Company and from then on were under the Crown.

When I joined there were about forty-five British infantry battalions in India. Under the so-called Cardwell System, each British infantry regiment had two battalions, one of which would be at home in England while the other was abroad somewhere – in India, Aden or the West Indies, for example – and every ten years they would change over. In the 1930s there was a strategic requirement for the presence of British troops in India; for this reason the British Government paid the costs of all British units in India to the Government of India. Britain also paid some of the cost of the

Indian Army too, again because it was part of the Empire's strategic reserve.

Russia, even in those days, was causing trouble around the world and there was always the threat of Russian expansion through Afghanistan and the Khyber Pass to the Indian Ocean. Therefore, in my day the bulk of the army, both British and Indian, was in the north, though other units were stationed all over India.

In addition to their strategic reserve role, all units in India were required to undertake internal security duties. There was always a certain amount of trouble, chiefly religious conflict, but after 1857 there was very little agitation against British rule. This was true even during the Second World War when the Indian Congress was agitating against India's participation. In 1947 at the partition of British India into independent India and Pakistan, the poor soldiers had the most miserable time trying to stop wholesale massacres, mainly on the borders of the new states: Hindu versus Muslim and vice versa, or Muslim versus Sikh and vice versa.

One must remember that British India was a large and partly unsettled country, about two-thirds the size of the United States. Communal riots were a common occurrence. Often started as the result of some fancied insult, they flared up with frightening speed. For example, the butchers of India were all Muslim and mostly they slaughtered sheep and goats, with the occasional buffalo. Relations between religious groups might be fragile in certain neighbourhoods and it only took the dissemination of a rumour that the butchers had slaughtered a cow (sacred to the Hindus) for a first-class riot to start, followed by indiscriminate killings on both sides.

The largest and most important unsettled territory was the North West Frontier (NWF) particularly along the border with Afghanistan. This unsettled belt of land, one hundred miles wide and more in places, stretched from a little north of the Khyber Pass way down towards Karachi just below Baluchistan. The inhabitants were all of the Pathan race, Muslim by religion. Proud and fiercely religious, their codes of behaviour were very strict and insults were repaid in blood. Every male adult owned a rifle and violent feuds were common. Sometimes a feud could be terminated by adjudication by tribal elders (*jirga*) and payment of substantial 'blood money', but not often.

The tribal areas in which they lived were mountainous and travel was extremely difficult. The stony land supported no crops worth the name. The tribes subsisted on grants of money from the British, who also allowed them to graze their herds of goats and camels in the settled (British) lands at the foot of their mountain fortresses. Some were employed as armed semi-regular police in tribal areas, but most of them had no allegiance to the British and no respect for British laws. Along the Frontier there were continual incidents of lesser or greater degree: from isolated murders of government officials to full-scale raids, not only for the booty they sometimes yielded, but often just for the hell of it.

Troops stationed on the Frontier lived on a permanent active service basis. Conditions were somewhat similar to those pertaining in the United States before the subjugation of the American Indian tribes. The Pathans' freelance attitude and addiction to raiding the settled areas of British India made them an excellent vehicle for propaganda from the Afghans, who came from similar stock. Afghanistan fostered political unrest with grants of money and supplies of weapons and ammunition. The Frontier was a perpetually simmering cauldron and no one knew where or when it would erupt into scalding steam.

I have mentioned that the British allowed the tribesmen to graze their herds in settled and semi-settled areas. The Kajauri plain where I was to fight my first battles, just north of Peshawar near the Khyber Pass, was one of the favourite grazing areas. The operations of 1930 were conducted to deny them this grazing as a punishment for some misdemeanour. At the time, there had been a lot of unrest and the Indian Congress Party was just beginning to gain strength, agitating for more Indian control of Indian affairs. Certain politicians made provocative speeches and sent out messages and money to encourage the tribesmen to give us trouble. This they felt aided them in their overall policy: to disrupt the government of the land. The Congress Party was not a militant party; on the whole it was nonviolent, but some party members did play around with the susceptibilities of the tribesmen and did not much care that the latter would indeed react violently.

One sultry evening at the beginning of the hot weather we were playing polo when suddenly we received orders to mobilize. Many of the men had left for their annual furlough and several of the officers were on leave. Dozens of telegrams were sent commanding instant return to duty. The horses had been 'let down' for the hot weather, which means they were unshod and were exercised daily in groups, tied together and without riders; they were ready for duty but were not as fit as if the riders had been there to exercise and groom them. Every single animal had to be shod 'all around', i.e. with horseshoes on all four feet. What's more, each horse had to have two full sets of shoes: one set affixed to his feet and the other set placed in special leather carriers suspended from the horse's saddle. Every squadron had its complement of farriers, but many were on leave and a large number of horses had to be shod very quickly. Headquarters of the 2nd Cavalry Brigade sent us every farrier available – British shoesmiths from the 9th Queen's Royal Lancers and 'The Eagle Troop', Royal Horse Artillery, as well as farriers from the Veterinary hospital and the mule companies. Everyone pitched in as officers and other ranks from all units of the brigade came to help the 6th Lancers mobilize.

Within forty-eight hours we were ready; all the multitudinous details had been checked and equipment packed. But where were we going? No one knew, not even the Colonel or Brigade HQ. There were rumours of a colossal tribal rising all along the Frontier, even stories of an Afghan invasion. In the bazaar it was whispered that a regiment had mutinied in Peshawar. The only concrete fact was that two long special trains were waiting for us at Sialkot railway station.

In the lines all was bustle, men were cursing and horses were neighing and stamping their feet. All were loaded with war equipment. Each trooper's horse, in addition to his bridle and reins, had a length of white picketing rope around his neck, with a loop at one end and a toggle at the other; these could be linked together and tethered with iron pegs – carried on each saddle – so that all the horses could be 'stabled' in the open. Under the saddle was a horse blanket and over it was a surcingle which could be used to hold the blanket on the animal's back when the saddle had been removed. On the front pommel two leather wallets contained the rider's personal kit. Lashed on top was a waterproof groundsheet to be worn by the rider in rainy weather or placed beneath his bedding when the ground was wet. At the back of the saddle was a bulky roll consisting of the rider's blanket and topcoat. Suspended from the saddle were the stirrups and irons. Attached to the iron on the 'off' (right) side was the small leather bucket to hold the butt of the lance; on the same side and to the rear of the stirrup, the large leather bucket contained the trooper's rifle. On the opposite side, balancing the rifle as it were, was a frog containing spare horseshoes and a loop through which was suspended the rider's sword, in a steel scabbard. Quite a load, even for a robust cavalry horse – but that was not all he had to carry. His rider stood at his head, ready to mount when ordered.

The rider also was loaded with equipment. The trooper wore black ankle boots, khaki puttees, breeches and shirt. Around his waist and across his chest was a Sam Browne-type crossbelt from which hung a haversack, a canteen containing dry rations and a full water bottle. On top of this, diagonally across his torso he wore a leather bandolier containing ninety rounds of rifle ammunition. In his right hand he held his lance, but as we were going on service the gay red-and-white lance pennons had been discarded and put in the heavy baggage. Again, quite a load – and, when one remembers that all of this was to be mounted on the horse's back in addition to all he was already carrying, commanders had to be very careful and considerate of the amount of work demanded of the horses. Most movements were done at a steady walk or trot; there was no light-hearted galloping down the highway, à la Hollywood; all was very precise. We did gallop sometimes, of course, but only for a specific purpose and for limited distances.

So we marched the two or three miles to Sialkot station. All the platforms had been decorated by our friends in the brigade. A hot meal and tea was ready for the men, after the horses were loaded into the wagons, and a huge buffet supper and bar for the officers. Throughout the evening the band of the 9th Queen's Royal Lancers played on the platform. But we still had no idea where we were going, except that initially the trains could only go westward to the junction at Wazirabad. Here the branchline from Sialkot joined the main north-south network. After that we could only guess.

The scene was reminiscent of pictures one had seen of troops leaving Victoria station in London on the outbreak of the First World War. All very romantic and exciting! Our hosts were somewhat envious of our selection to be the first to meet whatever threat there was, but were consoled by the thought that the rest of the 2nd Cavalry Brigade would probably follow us in short order. Quite obviously a threat of some magnitude had arisen. It could not be simply to suppress a communal disturbance that we were being moved; in those cases, the police were involved long before troops were sent for and therefore we would have read of the incident in the daily newspapers. Since 1919 tribal incursions along the Frontier had never been on a scale to warrant reinforcements from so far afield; and, for various reasons, we discounted the rumours of disaffection in army units. There were normally sufficient troops along the Frontier to deal with any such eventuality. So, we reasoned, it must either be an insurrection on a large scale or more likely an attack from across the border. We left in high spirits.

Our destination, it eventually turned out, was Peshawar, capital of the North West Frontier Province. As I had discovered the year before, Peshawar was a large and densely populated city, terminal for all trade to the north with Afghanistan. Adjoining the city was Peshawar Cantonment, where British civilians lived alongside an infantry brigade, some artillery and a cavalry regiment. The total area of the cantonment and city was contained within a barbed-wire perimeter, except for certain modern installations such as the ordnance depot which had their own local protection. The gates of the perimeter were closed at sunset.

Peshawar was only a few miles from the Afridi tribal border and it had become a common sight to see small groups of armed Afridis going about their business in the city. Provided their numbers were limited, they were allowed to pass freely during daylight hours, but they had to be back in tribal territory well before dark. Then, in 1930, the Afridi tribesmen began to infiltrate the city on a large scale, raiding and looting and causing unrest;

and this, coupled with widespread political agitation, was the reason for our sudden mobilization.

As usual, the Indian Congress Party was behind the political activity. Up to now, the tribesmen and the Pathans had despised the Congress Party and had shown no particular political ambitions; besides, the NWF Province was a traditionally Muslim area and the Congress Party was predominantly Hindu. But the Congress Party had enlisted the support of a Pathan, Khan Abdul Gaffar Khan, who formed a new party called *Khudai Khidmagars* (Servants of God), popularly known as 'Red Shirts'. The Red Shirts, with their headquarters at the remote town of Charsadda, belonged to the Muslim faith; but they shared with the Congress Party a policy of civil disobedience. Theoretically non-violent, they were at times very violent indeed. They staged marches and massive demonstrations, interrupted telephone and telegraph lines, burned down post offices and generally attempted to provoke the local population to unrest.

Between the Red Shirts and the Afridi tribesmen, the Peshawar garrison had its hands full. Indeed, on one occasion, the Peshawar cavalry regiment, the 17th Poona Horse, had nearly lost two Vickers machine guns to the tribesmen. The troopers had been watering their horses when the Afridis burst out of the tall crops surrounding the cantonment at that time of year and attempted to seize the guns. Fortunately one of their officers, Captain Newall, and his orderly had still been mounted; without hesitation, Captain Newall charged the guns and skewered the nearest tribesman. The others beat a fast retreat into cover and the situation was saved. But this incident demonstrates that the tribesmen, who had previously avoided confrontations with horsemen, were becoming very bold.

In fact, every garrison along the Frontier was fully occupied with similar raids. The authorities were in danger of losing control. Such was the danger that the newspapers had been forbidden to report the troubles, lest they cause similar unrest in other areas. Even in the Army, reasons of security had prevented dissemination of any news about the situation – at our level, at any rate.

But now the authorities had decided to call in reserves from further south.

7

Red Shirts and Afridis

The two special trains, after being switched at Wazirabad junction, chug-chugged slowly north towards the Frontier and Afghanistan. We passed through Jhelum and Rawalpindi, our progress so unhurried that even the mail trains were overtaking us. Despite the urgency of our move, the North Western Railway considered that normal scheduled traffic took precedence over our trains.

Eventually we reached yet another junction, only some thirty miles from Peshawar. There, to our surprise, our trains were switched to the north-west on the line that passed through Risalpur and Mardan. The former housed the 1st Cavalry Brigade, all of whom we learned were already out in the countryside. Mardan was the permanent home of that famous corps, the Queen Victoria's Own Corps of Guides. Based at this beautiful place for some eighty years, the Guides consisted of a cavalry regiment and an infantry battalion. Their mess was a veritable museum; in addition to regimental trophies and mementoes, it contained many relics of Alexander the Great's settlement at nearby Taxila. But when we arrived, late in the evening, the Guides too were out on deployment in the countryside.

The men and horses of the 6th Lancers were soon settled into the Guides' lines. After all had been attended to, the officers collected at the Guides' mess for whisky and a belated supper. It was well after 1 am when we had finished and I called for my orderly to find out where I was billeted. He led me along rambling paths and finally over a small drawbridge. As we approached the bungalow I noticed, on both sides of the path, row upon row of gravestones. Aiming my torch at the nearest rows, I saw to my amazement that most of them were the graves of Scottish soldiers killed in a Frontier War toward the end of the last century. Why they were buried in the garden of this house I never discoverd, but they gave me a very eerie welcome to my new quarters.

The following day we were briefed by the civil authorities on the Red Shirt party and its sphere of operations. The movement had started in Charsadda, about twenty miles west of Mardan, and had many followers throughout the district. Whenever police or troops were nearby they hid their red shirts – from which, of course, they got their name – and appeared as part of the local scene. Then, at an appointed signal, they would foregather elsewhere in hundreds and sometimes in thousands to terrorize the countryside. They demanded 'subscriptions' in cash and kind, and all those opposed to their politics were beaten up – in some cases murdered. They tried to interrupt all communications and set fire to outlying post offices and small police posts. On the day before we moved out from Mardan, a British Police officer, who had been trying to talk a large party of Red Shirts into returning to their homes peacefully, was brutally murdered during an apparently friendly discussion.

Our job was to round up the leaders of this movement and help the police to arrest those accused of the more serious crimes. This had to be done surreptitiously. The police network of spies and informers would report that Red Shirt leaders were based in a certain village and planning a raid in that area. The 6th Lancers would be briefed and either the whole Regiment or a squadron or two would move out after dark to surround the village. Then at first light the police could go in, either to make arrests or to flush out the people they were looking for into our surrounding cordon. These movements often entailed night-long marches across very broken country, for we had to avoid the main roads and tracks in the interest of secrecy.

Throughout the long hot summer of 1930, we were encamped in tents on the outskirts of Charsadda, and spent many long days and nights chasing these will-o'-the-wisps. We caught a few of their leaders, including the man alleged to have murdered the British police officer. He happened to land, almost literally, in my lap. We were searching a village about thirty miles from Charsadda. Dawn was breaking and I was sitting astride my horse, close against the wall of the village. Along the top of the wall were the backs of houses with small shuttered windows. Suddenly I heard a loud crash above me – and a body hurtled down onto my horse's neck. He, of course, reared up and, as we rolled on the ground, I saw the man had a curved sword in his hand. He tried to slash at me, then started to run towards the crops. Fortunately my orderly was nearby; seeing what was happening, he had time to draw his sword and give chase. The runaway did not get far. Fearing cold steel between his shoulder blades, he dropped his sword and surrendered. He was a bloodthirsty cuss and the police were delighted to have him in custody. He received a swift trial and ended up on the end of a rope in Peshawar jail. I still have his sword, which is an unusual pattern for the Frontier: whereas the traditional sword has a circular pommel, this sword has no hand guard and a Crusader-type 'cross' hilt; also it was made for a man with a very small hand.

The summer dragged on. Then in August we heard that men of the Afridi tribe had raided Peshawar in support of the Red Shirts; the tribesmen had infiltrated the cantonment and the old city in some numbers. Most of the local garrison was occupied elsewhere, so they had the place much to themselves for an hour or two. People were shot on the streets; an armoured car sent into the city unescorted was burnt and the crew killed. The most damage was done at the ordnance depot, a mile or so outside the perimeter, where the watchmen were overrun and several warehouses sacked and set on fire. By the time reinforcements arrived the tribesmen had slipped away to their own territory through the dense crops of cane, etc., which grew close to the city and cantonments.

This was too much for the Government of India. A tribal raid on a city as important as Peshawar – and in broad daylight too! It was unheard of. The Afridis had to be taught a lesson.

About ten miles south-west of Peshawar lies the Kajauri plain, shaped like a horseshoe and some hundred square miles in area. It is bounded on the western or tribal side by precipitous hills rising a thousand feet above the plain, on the north by the Besai Ridge, and on the south by the Bara River. In those days there was a rough track through Samgakki Pass, a gap in the Besai Ridge, running north towards Jamrud Fort at the eastern end of the Khyber Pass, while the southern entrance to the plain was dominated by the mud-walled Bara Fort, beside the river. But the key features of the plain, as far as our operations were concerned, were the prominent whale-backed hill in the centre of the horseshoe, Karawal as it was called, and a smaller hill to the east called the Batcha.

The whole area of the plain, split by steep-sided *nullahs* (gulches), was stony and covered with coarse grass and camel-thorn bushes. Every winter when the grass in their high mountain territory became sparse, the Afridi tribesmen would drive their herds of camels and goats down on to the plain and remain there until spring. But now, in retaliation for the raid on Peshawar, the Government of India decided to hit the tribesmen where it hurt most: by denying them their traditional grazing rights on the plain. Because the Afridis depended on the animals for their livelihood, it was judged that such a move would force the tribesmen into reconsidering their rash behaviour.

The plan was to send a whole infantry division, with the 6th Lancers as divisional cavalry, to occupy the plain and prepare for a move into tribal territory.

And so, one bright sunny morning in September, 1930, we packed up our camp on the outskirts of Charsadda and set off towards Peshawar. It was a delightful ride, although the dust was a nuisance. The road meandered through miles of high-standing crops irrigated by endless water channels fed by the great canal systems. The road itself was metalled but not macadamized, with a broad earthen berm on either side, and it was on these berms that we marched. After the hot, dry summer they quickly turned to powder as the passage of hundreds of horses churned them up. The dust cloud could be seen for miles, and all the men rode with the tail ends of their turbans wrapped across their noses and mouths. They looked like a gang of Tuareg tribesmen from the Sahara Desert. Trailing along behind the squadrons was the regimental transport and its escort: miles and miles of tiny AT (animal transport) carts, each drawn by two small mules side by side with the driver sitting on top of the load. These carts were really very uneconomical, as they held a very small load, but they were narrow and their hardworking mules could pull them almost anywhere – even across country.

On arrival at Peshawar we were met by a staff officer who directed us to the Peshawar racecourse, which was to be our billet for about three weeks. A delightful interlude. The officers' mess was in the grandstand and there was plenty of shade for men and horses. Work was cut to a minimum. All weapons were checked and repaired or replaced where necessary.

In the mornings one had a pleasant ride around the racecourse and later in the day repaired to the Peshawar Club. The station was crammed with troops. I had never seen the concentration of a whole division; there were hundreds of officers from every branch of the service and all ready to have a good time before getting the job done. Many ladies had returned from their hilltop summer resorts and the club was the scene of various activities almost the whole day and night long – tennis, squash, concerts, dances and amateur theatricals. The whole scene was one of great festivity, perhaps the thought of expected action lending spice to the occasion. I remember seeing a cryptic notice on the club bulletin board one Sunday morning after a particularly hectic Saturday night dance: 'Will the lady who left her bag and "bags" in my car last night please contact Colonel X . . .' Seems there had been some activity in the car park as well as on the dance floor! The long bar was packed at all hours and it was said that enough money was made in one

50

month to pay off all the Club's debts and to redecorate practically every room in the place.

But all good times have to end, and the day came when the 6th Lancers received orders to move foward. Our new base was to be Bara Fort.

8

Charge!

Bara Fort was a good deal less comfortable than Peshawar racecourse – particularly when the tribesmen started shooting at us at night. We had to dig trenches so that our sleeping cots were three or four feet below ground level; but the poor old horses had to weather the storm outside, tied by the headstall to the long picketing ropes and hobbled by one hind leg. Luckily we didn't get too many horses or men hit at that stage, for the shooting was really just indiscriminate long-range harassment by small-arms fire.

In mid-October we were ordered to move onto the Kajauri plain and clear the area of any tribesmen. So we left camp one morning with the Hindu and Muslim squadrons in the lead and the Sikh squadron in reserve. At a steady trot we headed for the great hump of Karawal hill.

To begin with there was no opposition, but then our CO, John Dick-Lauder, focused his fieldglasses on the area of the Samgakki Pass, apparently having seen some movement there. He gave me half the Sikh squadron, two troops, and told me to check out the pass and make sure the tribesmen didn't come down the track to outflank the advancing regiment.

Delighted to be let loose on my own, I duly set off with my sixty or seventy troopers and a signaller to communicate with regimental HQ. We crossed the broken ground with scouts out in front and the troops well spread out to present the smallest target to enemy fire. On reaching the Samgakki Pass, however, we found no sign of the enemy. After a careful search I rode up to the top of the pass with a couple of troopers. Again there was nobody there. So the signaller set up his lamp and started to tick-tack his message back to HQ, two or three miles away, reporting 'All clear'.

Suddenly I saw them: hundreds upon hundreds of tribesmen. It was like a scene from *Beau Geste*. The hills seemed to be swarming with them, yelling and shouting like crazy, waving multicoloured banners, beating tom-toms and firing rifles in the air. Some of them had *jezails*, old-fashioned guns with great long barrels that fired a ball weighing about eight ounces – when it shot through the air it made a sort of whoosh like a cannonball, rather than a sharp crack like a rifle bullet.

Outnumbering us by about ten to one, they started to encircle us, shooting from all directions. One or two of the horses were hit, none of them seriously but they were kicking up a hell of a fuss. Then the signal lamp was hit; we could no longer communicate with the rest of the Regiment. My men were doing their best, firing back at the tribesmen in an effort to stave off their advance, but we were heading for a one-sided fight in unsuitable terrain. I decided we should move out.

The tribesmen were already filtering down the ridge and on to the plain where there was plenty of cover for them to ambush us. Explaining my plan to the two troop leaders, I pointed to a stony outcrop on Karawal hill and told them to ride straight for it; if the enemy tried to cut us off we should gallop right through them. Then I formed up the two troops, side by side in line, and took my place at the centre with my trumpeter close behind me.

Away we went at a nice steady trot: eight miles an hour, bump, bump, bump. None of that cowboy-film stuff with horses galloping full out! Except when it's necessary for the charge, a cavalry regiment moves only at a walk or a trot, or sometimes at a canter, for this is the only way to ensure cohesion and discipline. But sitting atop a horse at this speed, I felt as big as a barn door with those characters shooting at me.

Then, to my surprise, for the Afridis didn't usually tangle with cavalry when they were mounted, about twenty or thirty of them appeared to our front, shooting directly at us. They were all in a state of great excitement, waving their flags in the air as bold as brass. Perhaps they thought they'd got us on the run. There was only one thing to do. 'Draw swords!' I shouted to the two troop leaders, and on this order the troops took their lances out of the buckets and pointed them towards the enemy. This was all done while we were still at a trot. Then I gave the signal to gallop.

The ground was not of the best, broken and rocky. As we galloped forward we jumped large holes in the ground and broken watercourses. Despite these diversions, we kept our direction on the objective and our speed increased. But still the enemy held their ground.

'*Charge!*' I yelled at the top of my voice, and put my sword down. Some of the men got excited and as a result their horses began to break ranks; but on the whole cohesion was good and we galloped right through the tribesmen.

They threw themselves to the ground, taking what cover they could, but a couple of them on the flanks got the feel of cold steel.

Admittedly we didn't do much damage, but the object was to get to a certain point intact. Well-trained troops do not go off chasing the enemy all over the countryside; if they are allowed to do so, cohesion is lost and somebody gets in trouble. In these circumstances a cavalry unit should stay 'knee to knee' if possible. In this manner, they should go through most opposition and come out the other side in good order – which, in fact, was what happened on this occasion.

When I judged it safe to do so, I held up my sword to slow the troops to a trot again. Many of the horses were neighing and blowing hard. There was still some desultory firing, but the troops soon settled down and we continued at a steady trot. Finally we reached the rest of the regiment on Karawal and I for one was very happy to be back.

But even on Karawal we were far from safe. Later that same day the tribesmen closed in on us again. I was on the forward side of the hill, talking to Jock White who commanded B Squadron, when suddenly there was a whoosh like an express train as a musket ball passed right between us. On the rock behind it left a great splat of lead, quite soft. It would have taken your head off at the roots.

Eventually, as the fire continued, we were ordered to withdraw. We were just clearing the Batcha, the smaller hill to the east of Karawal, when there was the sudden chatter of a light machine gun further up the hill. This came as quite a surprise to us for the tribesmen had never previously used any LMGs; afterwards we heard they were Belgian light automatics which the Afghans had acquired and passed on to the Afridi tribesmen. So a squadron of our men turned round to retake the Batcha, supported by mountain artillery.

I was fascinated to watch the antics of the artillery battery as it went into action. (Not that I knew it then but I was watching a little bit of history, for their guns were the immediate successors to the famous screw guns of Kipling's day and they fired a two-pound projectile over about one mile; very shortly afterwards they were made obsolete, replaced by the excellent 3.7-inch howitzer. The guns were carried on big strapping mules, about fourteen hands high, most of which came from either the Argentine or the Middle West of the United States. The men were all dismounted, leading the mules by a rope, and they doubled forward with a great rattling and flapping. But it was a very well groomed battery and the mules were steady under fire.

When they reached a forward position, they stopped and the mules stood still while the gear was dismounted. First the guns were taken off: one man took the wheels, another the trail and a third the barrel. The three pieces were quickly married together with pins in slots, then men ran forward with the ammunition and stacked it beside the guns. Meanwhile the section commander was giving fire orders and the gunners began to train their guns on the targets. The loaders rammed shot into the breech of each gun – then the guns began to fire.

Their effectiveness was partly thanks to a young officer on horseback who acted as a forward observer. I saw him ride about 300 yards away to one flank, then stop and sit there with his glasses up to his eyes. I never did find out how he got any information back to the gunners, but he obviously did for the squadron had soon done the job, and with very few casualties too.

I don't believe there are any pack artillery units left in the British or US Armies, but a large number were used during the Second World War, particularly in Burma where they carried 3.7-inch howitzers. We could have done with some in Europe. When we were dismounted in the Apennine Mountains in Italy there was a Cypriot mule outfit backing our regiment; they were not combat troops, however, and carried only ammunition and other supplies. There were times when I wished they packed three-seven hows!

Not that we knew it then, of course, but this particular operation of 1930 was the last big battle on the Frontier, though there was another blow-up in 1935. A medal was awarded for Frontier campaigns and I duly received one of them: the India General Service Medal. The ribbon was green and dark blue and suspended from it was a silver medal with King George V's head on one side and a fort on a hilltop on the reverse. For each campaign, ever since the medal had been struck in 1908, there was a different clasp; in our case the clasp was engraved 'North West Frontier 1930–31'.

The 1935–36 operation was further north, in the Mohmand country, and included one famous action involving the Queen Victoria's Own Corps of Guides. An isolated company of the Guides commanded by Captain Godfrey Meynell was cut off on a hilltop by vast numbers of tribesmen; the battle raged for twenty-four hours but finally the Guides were overrun. Every last man of them was killed, including Captain Meynell. When the relieving troops arrived, the enemy dead outnumbered the strength of the company by ten to one. For his gallantry Captain Meynell was post-humously awarded the Victoria Cross.

The British Army is very sparing with its honours and awards; in the 1930 operation the only medal for gallantry that I know of was awarded to 'Daddy' Newall who was given the Military Cross. Yet I saw many other examples of gallantry that went unrewarded, despite the ferocious fighting when our men had to face the Afridi tribesmen of the North West Frontier.

9

Beer, Puttees and Patronymics

After the action against the tribesmen was over, we packed up and withdrew to Bara Fort, while the infantry moved on to Karawal. To this day the post built there is known as Fort Salop, named after the King's Shropshire Light Infantry, the British unit which consolidated the area. It took some days to clear the plain because the tribesmen were continually popping up in unexpected places, but gradually the influx of soldiery made it impossible for them to get too far down on our side of the plain.

Three brigade camps were formed: one at Bara Fort, another at Karawal and a third much deeper into tribal territory at Miri Khel, a tribal hamlet close by. Here a brigade group was encamped. By day they moved around the area with patrols and sorties, generally denying the area to the tribesmen. One of the battalions at Miri Khel was the Argyll and Sutherland Highlanders, a very famous Scottish regiment that I had the privilege of fighting alongside in the Second World War. At this time they were commanded by a delightful gentleman named John Hay. I didn't know him very well, since he was much my senior, although subsequently I did sell him a horse!

The Argylls were all Scotsmen from the Highlands, recruited from the area around Fort William – the British Army in those days was very territorial – and, like British soldiers everywhere, they enjoyed their beer. They didn't have much in the way of entertainment, particularly in this remote hamlet, but they did have their beer. So as soon as the brigade had settled in at Miri Khel, the Argylls erected a 'wet canteen'. This was a large tent, some sixty feet long, with row upon row of tables inside and Indian servants to carry their drinks. The beer – spirits were never permitted to other ranks – was imported, of course, for India did not have a brewing industry worth the name.

One evening after dark, when the Jocks were packed into the wet canteen, some tribesmen decided that this large dimly lit tent was the perfect target. From their vantage point in the foothills, several hundred yards away, they started shooting at the camp, concentrating on the canteen tent. Even at that distance, their bullets easily pierced the canvas roof and walls.

Inside the wet canteen there was pandemonium as the Jocks scrambled to get out, tripping over tables and colliding with the Indian servants. Soon the great tent was empty save for one man – Private McTavish – and scores of unattended bottles of beer. McTavish wore an expression of utter astonishment: no one deserts a beer, even when fired upon! Dutifully he finished his own beer, then, moving ever faster, seized the next bottle and emptied its contents down his throat, then the next, and the next . . . until he reached the far end of the tent. By this time more than half seas over, he staggered out of the wet canteen slap into the arms of the Regimental Police Corporal.

'Heh! Mind where ye're going, McTavish! Where the hell have ye been?'

'Weel, Corporal, I've been fighting the bluidy Afridis, tha's wha' I been doin', while yon lily-livered buggers ran awa'.'

'Oh ye have, have ye? From the smell of yer breath they must have been firing beer at you.'

'Tha's reet, McEwan's it wor too. Hic!'

'That's enough for tonight, McTavish,' said the Corporal. 'Ye're under arrest.'

By this time the gallant McTavish had subsided to the ground and was ignominiously removed to the guard tent to cool off. The following day, when he was sober (because you never try anybody when he's drunk), he was brought up before his Company Commander who considered the offence sufficiently serious to remand him to the Commanding Officer. He was arraigned before Colonel John Hay and charged with being drunk and disorderly.

Colonel Hay asked McTavish what he had to say. He answered that he had nothing to say, except that he'd thought it a shame to see all that good beer abandoned and so he drank it. He really wasn't excusing himself, but simply explaining that it had seemed to him the proper thing to do at the time. John Hay considered the situation. McTavish was a good soldier, steady if not brilliant, and always ready to do his duty. The Colonel looked him over and said, 'Very well, McTavish, you are admonished and that will be recorded. However, I'm also going to write a special report and send it to the Brigadier recommending you for presence of mind under fire. Case dismissed!'

Another incident, in my own Regiment, concerned a soldier like McTavish: a good soldier but again not awfully bright. His name was Waryam Singh; like all Sikhs, his last name was Singh, meaning lion. This is a part of their religious system. We had several Waryams in the squadron and we had to differentiate between them in some way, so they were known as 'Waryam Singh 05', or '04' or whatever were the last numerals of their regimental number. Hardly any of the other ranks in the Indian Army had surnames; they were all Khan or Singh or Ram.

One day we were preparing to move out of camp to go into the plain when I heard a disturbance in the lines. I walked towards the Sikh squadron where the men were saddling the horses, getting ready to leave. On this occasion the altercation involved Waryam Singh, who was often the butt of practical jokers. It seemed that he had lost one of his puttees. (A puttee was worn by the cavalry soldier between his breeches and his boots. There was one for each leg: a long strip of cloth which was wound around the calf with a tape to tuck in at the bottom.) Waryam Singh had a puttee on one leg only; the other leg was bare from the breeches end down, with a sock sticking up out of his boot. He looked distinctly lopsided. He was cursing and shouting that somebody had stolen his other puttee, and accusing his best friend who slept in the same tent. But we couldn't hold back the whole squadron because one man had lost a puttee, and finally we rode off to attend to our duties on the plain.

Poor Waryam Singh; all day long he suffered the ribbing and laughter of his companions because he had one leg naked, but clearly he was not amused. At last the day was over and we returned to Bara Fort. The men unsaddled and watered their horses and put the nosebags on for the evening feed, then returned to their quarters to relax, removing their breeches and boots and putting on lightweight pyjamas. Both literally and figuratively they let their hair down. Sikhs, who favour long hair for religious reasons, take off their turbans and let their long hair go loose when they're having a rest. Suddenly I heard a loud burst of laughter and, going to investigate, found Waryam Singh standing in the middle of a group of men and looking very shame-faced. He was still wearing his breeches, one calf covered with the puttee, the other calf naked – but in his hand he held the other puttee. He had wrapped two around the same leg!

From then on, Waryam Singh 08 became Waryam Singh Puttee. I have often wondered whether today, nearly fifty years later, there is not a family somewhere round Ludhiana enjoying the patronymic of Puttee! After all, how did the Anglo-Saxon names Smith, Barber or Wheelwright originate?

Our job was more or less finished after the Karawal clearing operation. The infantry had taken over and we remained in camp at Bara Fort for a few days. Then we were told that, having had such a hard summer, we would be permitted to return to our own station at Sialkot. This meant that we could get down to the serious business of life, preparing to play in the winter polo tournaments; the Christmas tournaments in Lahore were particularly inviting. We were relieved at Bara Fort by the Peshawar cavalry regiment, the 17th Poona Horse, but I doubt if they had much to do because the plain was already in the hands of the infantry.

Just before we left Bara Fort we were visited by a very famous soldier, the Commander-in-Chief in India, Field-Marshal Lord Birdwood. He had risen to fame in the South African War and at Gallipoli in the First World War. Lord Birdwood was a cavalryman and took particular interest in my regiment. He had come to see what was happening in the plain and, of course, talked to the men. He was a very paternal figure, a charming man with a phenomenal memory for names and faces; but, as we were to discover, he didn't like having his leg pulled.

In charge of the water supply at Bara Fort was an engineer officer named Adami who was something of a wag. Knowing the Commander-in-Chief was interested in everybody's welfare, Adami told the local brigadier that he had just completed a new 'water-borne system' and he asked if the Commander-in-Chief would come and open it. This sounded a reasonable enough request and so, not giving too much thought to the matter, the brigadier agreed. When Lord Birdwood arrived, followed by a retinue of generals and staff officers all strung out behind him like a gaggle of geese, he was conducted to the top of the bluff overlooking the Bara river. And there, perched atop the cliff, was a small hut which everyone assumed to be part of a pumping station or something equally technical. Stretched across the door was a broad red ribbon, and beside it stood Major Adami with a pair of shears in his hand.

Adami gave the Field-Marshal a chance to inspect the site, looking down at the river and asking questions about the sufficiency and quality of the water. Then Adami saluted him very smartly and, handing him the shears, asked him: 'Sir, would you be kind enough to open our water-borne system?'

Had anyone thought about it, they would soon have realized that the 'water-borne system' was nothing more than a portable latrine. Inside the little hut was a cistern with a bucket and chain. But, all unsuspecting, the Commander-in-Chief stepped forward and cut the ribbon, then opened the door and went inside. I am not sure whether he actually pulled the chain or not, but when he backed out and turned to face the tittering lines of staff officers, he certainly did not look as if he'd found the episode very entertaining!

Finally the day came when we left Bara Fort. Again we travelled by train and had to load our resisting horses into the covered railway wagons. The horses hated the wagons and the crashing, shunting and banging as the trains moved; you could hear them kicking the iron wagon sides. But at last we reached Sialkot and a warm welcome from the 13th/18th Hussars, who had relieved the 9th Queen's Royal Lancers in our absence. They had arranged a band and a buffet at the station and a big dance that night at the club. It was to be the start of a winter's socializing.

10

Furlough, Fun and Polo

The Army virtually packed up over the Christmas season; everybody got ten days' leave and went off to have fun. Leave was easy in those days. In addition to the occasional 'ten-dayer', an Indian Army officer was entitled to two months' leave on full pay each year, and eight months' furlough every third year. The 'long leave' as we called it was only granted to regular officers of the Indian Army, to keep them in touch with their homeland and to compensate for the 'rigours of the Indian climate'. Indeed, nearly everyone spent their long leave in England – particularly as the Government met the cost of the return passage. When an officer joined, the Government opened a special 'passage account' of several hundred pounds, which was meant to last one's whole service in the Army. One therefore had a choice: whether to sail first-class and blow the lot in three or four visits home, or go second-class and spread the fund over a longer period. In the 1930s the Italians put a beautiful ship on the Bombay–Italy run, the MV *Victoria*, which had a class called *seconda economica*; moderate in price and with good accommodation, many people chose to use this service.

The annual two months' leave had to be spent in India. This was no hardship, however, as there was so much to do, so many places to go and people to meet. In the hot weather it was a relief to go to the hill country, to places like Kashmir where one could fish or play golf at Gumarg's two beautiful mountain golfcourses, or to Simla or one of the other hill stations in the Himalayan foothills. The ladies in particular tended to enjoy Kashmir, away from the heat of the plains. In fact the ladies themselves were one of the chief attractions of the hill stations – though if a young officer went

61

chasing off after them too often, he became liable to a charge of 'poodle-faking'!

One could get ten days' leave several times a year, except during regimental or brigade training; and, just to put cream on the cake, one could ask for three days' casual leave at any time. Naturally there were limitations; no CO approved of unlimited leave and one had to have a 'reason'. Poodle-faking was out, but one of the best 'reasons' was a commitment to play polo for a regimental team.

At Christmas the station was left in the hands of a small caretaker party while the rest of us took our ten days off. The ten days might start on a Saturday but it wouldn't count until Monday, since Saturdays and Sundays were both holidays; Thursday, too, was a holiday in the Indian Army – because Queen Victoria had proclaimed herself Empress of India on a Thursday – so only Monday, Tuesday, Wednesday and Friday were full working days. But, strange to relate, we did work too, and hard.

One of the great delights of Christmas at Sailkot was that Lahore was the nearest city, and Lahore had much to offer, from English shops to polo tournaments. And in winter the weather was nice and cold.

In the north of India the climate is tolerable from late September to March or April; in fact for six months of the year the weather is gorgeous, rather like central California. We had warm sun by day but by nightfall it was cool enough to light the open fires. The summers, however, were very hot indeed and we had neither air conditioning nor refrigerators to ease our discomfort. Most houses would have an ice box, lined with lead, which contained a block of ice; this was collected daily from an ice factory in the bazaar, usually by the cook on a bicycle. The ice box helped to keep meat or butter fresh for a while. Butter, incidentally, was generally buffalo butter: white, with a high fat content, inclined to stick to the roof of your mouth and not very appetizing. Certain big military stations had their own dairies producing decent milk and butter, but if you were in a small place you had to live off the land. The meat was mostly chicken or goat and there were eggs in plenty, though very few fish from those rivers in northern India were fit to be eaten. In winter matters improved considerably when one had European vegetables grown by one's own gardener. The diet, in short, was simple but adequate.

Lahore, capital of the Punjab, had a big civil population as well as a military cantonment. In addition to the courts and government offices the city was home to the Punjab University and many other colleges and schools. It had two excellent clubs, the Punjab Club and the Gymkhana Club, and two good hotels, Faletti's and Nedou's. Old man Nedou was still alive in those days and his hotel was as old as he was – very Victorian. We poor soldiers considered the hotels too expensive to stay in, but they were fun places to go for a drink or a party.

The main street of Lahore was the Mall. Every station had its mall, a sort of refined high street, but Lahore's was particularly fine. Almost one hundred feet wide, it ran for miles through the Civil Lines – the civilian part of the city – and along the whole length were planted rows of stately plane trees. On one side there was a tanbark riding track and one could ride a horse right out of Lahore without ever crossing tarmac. Every winter the Public Works Department put down new tanbark so that it always looked tidy and groomed.

In the centre of the Civil Lines, facing down the Mall, was a splendid mansion: Government House, where His Excellency the Governor of the Punjab lived. On the upper part of the Mall were a number of English shops; these had no branches in outlying stations so one tended to save one's serious shopping for a trip to Lahore. The shops included a haberdashery, a jeweller's shop, a tailor's and a lovely confectionery-cum-coffee shop called Lorang's. Mr Lorang was a Swiss and he sold delicious cakes, coffee and tea; here one could sit and watch the world go by on the Mall.

Motor cars were few and far between in those days; most of the traffic was made up of *tongas*, the indigenous pony and trap, or bicycles. The streets were also thronged with pedestrians, from multi-hued coolies carrying loads on their heads to elegant foreigners strolling with their ladies. It was a kaleidoscopic picture.

Like the other big cities in northern India such as Delhi and Peshawar, Lahore was visited every winter by what was vulgarly termed 'the fishing fleet': young ladies who had come out from England to find a husband. They spent the season in one of the big centres, taking advantage of every social occasion, and in many cases they did indeed find suitable young men to marry. The social life of Lahore was particularly lively, with lots of parties and dances. The big dances were usually held at the Gymkhana Club, which had a huge ballroom; at one end of the ballroom, opposite the band, there were twin majestic staircases leading up to a gallery from which one could look down at the splendid colourful spectacle of ladies in fine ballgowns and officers in a variety of mess dress.

One of the most popular activities was going to the races. Lahore had a large racecourse with a pretentious grandstand and regular meetings took place here throughout the winter, controlled by the Royal Calcutta Turf Club. A number of young officers owned racehorses and rode them in flat races, although this was frowned upon by their superiors: 'Jones of the 99th? Yes, I know him – racing swine!' Oddly enough, though, it was considered perfectly acceptable to own and ride horses in the steeplechase races, which were run under gymkhana rules. I myself took part in a number of such races, and had my own horse – Eager Heart. Australian bred, he won a lot of races for me and became very well known; I also rode him when playing polo and going on parade. His picture, painted by Susan Terrot, my first wife, appears on the dedication page.

The main event of the big Christmas week race meeting was the Governor's Cup, which attracted some of the best performers on the flat. As colourful as Ascot, it was a great pageant. The Governor of the Punjab drove up the course in an open carriage drawn by camels and escorted by a squadron of cavalry. I once had the privilege of commanding this escort; the course was a beautiful sight as we rode past the rails lined with thousands of Indians from the bazaars and the stands packed with elegantly dressed ladies and gentlemen.

Another typically British occasion was the hunt, for Lahore even had its own pack of foxhounds. They used to meet early on Sunday mornings, at about 5 am, before the hot sun could destroy the scent. The quarry was rather second-rate, however – the jackal, which lacks both the courage and the endurance of the English red fox.

Much more to my taste was the game of polo.

In most cavalry regiments in India, polo took second place only to military training. All officers were expected to practise and study game strategy as well as schooling the ponies.

Although hardly known or understood outside horsey circles, polo is a thrilling game for both players and spectators. A full-sized ground is three hundred by two hundred yards, a vast expanse in which two opposing teams of four players each gallop and twist and turn at full speed. In our day the goals were light openwork bamboo slats covered with red and white cloth, designed to topple easily should a pony and rider crash into them at speed. The gap between the goalposts was narrow, a mere twelve feet, which called for great accuracy, particularly if one player was being ridden off (jostled) by another.

It could be a very aggressive game and there was tremendous rivalry between the various teams in India. Unfortunately only two of the three brigaded cavalry regiments were located near our station in Sialkot; the third was nearly two hundred miles away at Jullundur. However, there were other units of the brigade at Sialkot – a battery of horse artillery, a troop of sappers and miners, and several infantry battalions – and many of their officers were well mounted, so Sialkot was a lively polo centre.

All tournaments were played in a highly competitive spirit, culminating in the Indian Cavalry and Inter-Regimental championships. The latter included both British and Indian cavalry teams, whereas the former was exclusive to Indian Army regiments. The Indian Cavalry championship took place at Lahore during the great spring festival, when there was a huge horse show in the military enclave.

In India the polo grounds were beautifully kept, with close-cropped springy turf, often in the centre of the local racecourse – as at Lahore; in fact there were four polo grounds in the middle of the Lahore racecourse, for this was where all the big tournaments took place. At Christmas there were two tournaments: a four-chukker event for the low-handicap teams and a six-chukker unlimited handicap tournament called the Punjab Challenge Cup. This attracted not only regimental sides and teams from all the different States of India, but private teams as well. I played these tournaments many times, both for the 6th Lancers and for a remount team called the Wild Geese.

Altogether, Sialkot in the winter was a delightful station with lots of balls, parties and social events. I rapidly began to understand why I'd had to buy so many uniforms to bring to India, and also why social etiquette had featured on the curriculum at Sandhurst.

Balls, of course, called for formal dressing up in the evening uniform or 'mess dress'. The variety of mess dress at such events was stunning, particularly the Indian cavalry officers who looked positively exotic. From the lemon yellow of Skinner's Horse to the brilliant scarlet of the 19th King George V's Own Lancers, an artist's palette could not have reflected as many hues. The infantry, both British and Indian, were much more staid by comparison; they wore the regular 'bum-freezer' jacket, starched shirt with butterfly collar and black bow-tie, as did the British cavalry who by this time (the 1930s) had given up their colourful high-necked jackets.

In the 6th Lancers our mess dress was black and scarlet and topped with a cavalry cloak; dark blue, with a scarlet collar and lining, the cloak fell almost to the ankles. On our heads we wore a 'fore and aft' cap, a little black side-cap bound in gold with the regimental badge in front; the cap had to be worn precisely one inch above the right eye. Our black leather boots – we called them Wellington boots – were worn over the skintight trousers ('overalls') and had dress spurs which jingled as one walked. It was considered bad form to wear spurs when dancing, however, so most officers removed and pocketed them whenever venturing on to the dance floor; no lady likes to be jabbed in the leg while tripping the light fantastic. The short black jacket, over a high-necked scarlet waistcoat, was trimmed with scarlet facings and gold epaulettes two inches wide.

These epaulettes were a vital clue to etiquette, for on the coiled gimp were the badges of rank (a crown for a major, three stars for a captain, one little star for a second-lieutenant and so on) which helped one know how to

65

address an officer if one hadn't met him before. In both the British and Indian Armies, officer ranks fell into four categories: subalterns (second-lieutenants and lieutenants), captains, field officers (major to colonel) and general officers (brigadier and up). Socially all officers were addressed by their rank – 'How do you do, Captain Bell?' – except for subalterns who were called 'Mister' (although the rank was used in letters and official publications: one of those British idiosyncrasies so confusing to foreigners!).

Another uniform in constant use was the 'Blue Patrol'. The boots and overalls were the same as the mess dress, but instead of the waistcoat and short 'shell jacket' we wore a longer dark blue jacket which had a high collar and shoulder chains on which were inserted the badges of rank. These chains were draped over the side of the shoulder, across the collarbone and back up to the neck; they were a relic from the days when cavalry used the cutting sword and the chain could prevent your arm from being lopped off. A number of cavalry regiments, including my own, still wear them to this day.

Apart from the side-cap we wore with mess dress, our headgear included a peaked black cap and a turban. The black cap, with a wide red band round it and a patent leather peak, was worn when you were officer of the day and inspecting the guard. The turban, or *pagri*, was worn when you went on service. Quite a complicated affair, the *pagri* usually had to be tied by someone else. The material – a very fine cotton, almost a muslin – was many yards long and about a yard wide, but it had to be folded over and over until reduced to about four inches. This was wound round the head, starting above one ear, until a uniform sort of bulge was achieved on both sides, and to hold it in position on top of the head was placed a *kullah*, a pointed cap. One could remove the turban and replace it two or three times, but after that it began to look a little untidy and had to be redone. Even an expert took about fifteen minutes.

Mess dress was also worn for dinner in the mess every night except Sunday, when the dinner jacket and black tie was *de rigueur*, though relatively few officers dined in on Sundays. For summer the mess dress jacket was white, trimmed with dark blue, and a multicoloured cummerbund was worn round the waist.

In those days mess life tended to be pretty formal, though the cavalry was less straight-laced than the infantry or 'The Feet' as we called them. Each regiment had its own mess rules, and visitors were expected to exchange calling cards and courteous letters written in the third person. But the officers' mess is a peculiar institution, so perhaps it deserves a fuller description.

Most messes were of the same general pattern, usually located in a building much like an ordinary house but passed down from unit to unit as regiments were moved. As well as the usual offices the mess consisted of a dining-room, a large living-room known as the 'anteroom', games rooms and a hallway where visitors could leave their cards or sign the guest book.

In the 6th Lancers' mess the anteroom was comfortably furnished with deep leather armchairs and the walls were covered in memorabilia; it was rather like a London club. This was where officers would gather before dinner or come to relax at other times. There was even a fireplace where we could warm our backs in winter while enjoying a drink and discussing the day's polo.

The trophies, admittedly, did give the place the air of a museum. Several had been acquired by our predecessors in the 16th Bengal Lancers (amalgamated with the 13th in 1921 to form the 6th Lancers), who had been at the Siege of Peking in 1900, during the Boxer Rebellion. In those days looting was considered one of the victor's perquisites and they came back with all sorts of valuable treasures which now adorned our mess: cloisonné figures, Ming vases, Tang porcelain and several items from Peking's Temple of Heaven, including the throne of cushion, lavishly covered in seed pearls. They had even brought back the Emperor's umbrella!

The anteroom walls also boasted several collections of medals once awarded to previous members of the regiment; stamped with the rank and name of the recipient, these medals provided interesting glimpses into the regiment's history. Other trophies including some Egyptian medals captured at the Battle of Tel-el-Kebir in 1882.

Leading off the anteroom through big double doors was the dining-room, again adorned with trophies – silver statuettes on the table, game trophies on the walls. As we sat at the long highly polished mahogany table, which could be extended to accommodate fifty people, the heads of deer, wild sheep and other animals leered down from above our heads, and over the fireplace hung a gigantic piece of ivory. Inscribed on this huge elephant tusk was the date it was shot and the name of the man who shot it: Colonel V. M. Stockley, who served in the 16th Bengal Lancers in the early part of the twentieth century and whose exploits are enshrined in Roland Ward's *Book of Records*.

The mess had a permanent staff of servants. In charge was the mess sergeant, an NCO from the regiment who was given the Indian rank of *duffadar*. He looked after the cooks and all the other mess staff and was responsible to the mess secretary. All junior officers took turns being mess secretary; it was very good training in housekeeping and how to budget because one's brother officers always grilled one if the cost of 'messing' rose even a few annas a day.

The mess *duffadar* (sergeant) and lance-*duffadar* (corporal) would stand at each end of the dining-room to oversee the dinner arrangements. Behind each officer's chair stood his bearer, who was responsible for serving his own master alone. The mess servants wore a white pyjamas-type uniform: a long white jacket with close-fitting white jodhpurs, and a cummerbund in the regimental colours of red, blue and silver. They also wore white cotton gloves to serve dinner.

Attending to the wine and liquor department was the *abdar*, or wine waiter, a dignified figure who responded to every call of *'Koi hai!'* Literally this means 'Who's there?' but the expression had become the usual way of calling for service. *'Hazoor,'* he would say by way of greeting (literally 'Your honour'), then bring the drink as ordered. He kept a record of everybody's individual consumption; even though there were no chits to sign he very rarely made a mistake.

Dinner was announced by a trumpet call half an hour before the dinner hour and again five minutes before. Then the mess *duffadar* would walk into the anteroom and, addressing the senior officer present, he would announce: *'Khana tiyar, hazoor'* (Dinner is served, sir).

On guest nights the arrangements were more formal. The trumpet calls were played by massed trumpeters and everyone was assigned his own place at the dining table. Usually there was one guest night a week when you might invite friends to dine with you. Once the dinner was over and the table cleared, two decanters of port were delivered to the 'President of the Mess', a senior officer sitting at the head of the table, and to the mess secretary at the other end, officiating as 'Vice-President' for the evening. The port would be passed clockwise round the table until everybody's glass was charged, then the President would stand and announce the loyal toast: 'Mr Vice – the King!'. This was the only toast we drank except on special occasions such as when a foreign diplomat was present; then we would offer a toast to the guest's country.

Smoking was prohibited until the port had been passed, as were risqué stories or talk about ladies. In those days nearly everyone smoked, either American cigarettes or Turkish ones known as 'Smellies'.

After dinner many officers retired to the games rooms. Most messes had a billiard room with a full-sized billiard table but we seldom played very seriously, preferring simple versions of the game like 'slosh'; practically anyone could score at slosh. Another game was 'billiard fives', but this was a rough game and didn't do the billiard table much good; it was generally forbidden if the mess had had a good dinner!

In summer the mess could be stifling. Even at night the temperature was about 98°F and the big-bladed fans overhead were not much help. As a result, many of us chose to sit outside in the evening air. The 6th Lancers' mess garden had overhead lights and fans, so it was a pleasure to sit out on the lawn among the formal flower beds and lots of pots and palms. The garden was well kept and watered and of course there was plenty of manure from the stables. In winter we had familiar English flowers such as stocks, pansies and sweet peas; but, much more typical of India, in summer the scents were those of frangipani and jasmine.

Scent can conjure up memories more instantly and evocatively than anything else. And yet the smell that I remember India for is not the haunting perfume of hot-weather flowers; it is the insidious, acrid, yet somehow attractive smell of cow-dung patties as the housewives built up their fires on which to cook the evening meal.

The winter was not entirely devoted to partying, however, for this was also the campaign season when regiments moved out of their station to go on manoeuvres. This meant that we all lived under canvas for a week or two, with long days and some nights spent in the saddle as we sharpened our tactics and techniques for war. But the al fresco living was an enjoyable change, particularly as every possible comfort was provided.

Each officer had his own personal tent, with bathroom attached. The tent alone weighed eighty pounds, on top of which we had to take all the contents: a camp cot, a *roorkee* (chair), a folding canvas table, a Petromax pressure lamp, several hurricane lamps called *bhattis* for the servants, and all our own gear as well. There was even a canvas tub.

Although each officer had his own 'jerry' in his bathroom in case a safety valve should be required after a riotous mess dinner, for one's more pressing early-morning needs one had to visit the Kitchener tents, strategically positioned downwind from the camp. These contained the usual commode or 'thunder box', the same type of facility one had in one's bungalow at Sialkot; with the exception of a few big houses in the cities and the occasional up-country hotel, British India had yet to learn the joys of the water closet. The name 'Kitchener tent' derives from circa 1900 when this facility was first introduced into the Army; a newspaper published a picture of said privy with a superimposed picture of General Kitchener standing alongside, and some wag had captioned it 'The latest general officer's accommodation provided by the Government.'

Even on manoeuvres we had to maintain standards: dinner was a four-course affair and we each had our own bearer with us as well as a military orderly. But the point of manoeuvres was that we should practise the arts of war, and this in itself was interesting as we were able to observe our friends from other units displaying their various skills.

I particularly remember the Royal Horse Artillery 'in action' on tactical exercises. Our artillery support in the 2nd Cavalry Brigade was 'N' Battery or The Eagle Troop as they preferred to be known. This honourable title dated back to the Battle of Waterloo when they captured one of Napoleon's Eagles – an outstanding exploit worthy of perpetual recognition. Their piece was the 13-pounder, soon to be obsolete. Although the gun and limber had iron-shod wheels, they were extremely mobile; their boast was that they could keep up with the cavalry at any speed and over any terrain.

The Eagle Troop team consisted of three pairs of Australian horses of the light draught variety. There were three riders on the near (left-hand) side horses. If needful they went like the hammers of hell, and a section of guns at full stretch was a magnificent sight. On one occasion the guns were coming into action at full gallop over an open piece of country. Suddenly a five-foot open ditch appeared in their path. They didn't pause. The lead drivers cracked their whips, and both teams surged towards the obstacle. There was no hesitation. Every pair of horses rose as one and sailed over the abyss, the guns and limbers bouncing high in the air as they hit the lip of the far bank. For co-ordination of man and beast, for sheer symmetry of motion, it is a memory to be treasured.

On another occasion I watched a gun team coming into action at dusk of a winter's eve, the horses galloping flat out along the tarmac of the Grand Trunk Road. The din and flying sparks would have done credit to Thor's smithy. What was it Kipling wrote? He's eulogizing the 'screw guns', but I feel it goes for all the Royal Artillery: *'They sends us where the roads are, but mostly we go where they ain't.'*

And so the winter passed, my first winter at Sialkot with the Bengal Lancers. Early in 1931, however, I found myself leaving Sialkot behind and departing on a very privileged assignment.

11

Kashmir

Sialkot cantonment is adjacent to the states of Jammu and Kashmir; indeed, the capital of the lesser state, Jammu, is only thirty miles from Sialkot. Here the ruler of both states, the Maharaja of Kashmir, spent the winter months. The Resident, a British civil servant who watched over and theoretically advised the Maharaja, spent the winter in Sialkot. But during the season, when the Vale of Kashmir is one of the beauty spots of the world, both His Highness and the Resident ensconced themselves in Srinagar; the Maharaja in his palace in the foothills surrounding Nageem Lake, the Resident in a smaller but no less princely house on the banks of the Jhelum River. The Residency was conveniently close to the European club, the golfcourse, the polo grounds and the only hotel in Srinagar, which was owned by the Nedou family – among the first hotel entrepreneurs in India.

During the winter the Resident was in semi-hibernation, so to speak. But in summer his life was one long round of diplomatic duties coupled with endless social functions. To enable him to handle this surfeit of socializing during his stay in Srinagar he was loaned the services of a junior army officer as personal assistant. The job was really just that of a glorified aide-de-camp, but delightful nonetheless – six months' poodle-faking on full pay! In 1931 the Resident was Colonel (later Sir) George Ogilvie; he asked our brigadier to recommend a young officer, and to my surprise it was my name that was proposed. I gratefully accepted.

It was the spring of 1931 when I arrived in Srinagar. It was so beautiful; all the Kashmiri houses, covered in turf to keep out the winter cold and rain, were now a never-ending ribbon of blue and white iris. The ground, warming in the spring sunshine, was a mass of crocus, jonquils and daffodils. The air was like wine and you could see for ever. I settled into a comfortable walnut-lined apartment over the western gatehouse. Here was a world of my own; no one to question my coming or going outside my regular duty hours. The extensive Residency gardens were laid out in the English style and reminded me so much of my home in England.

My duties were light and pleasant: I received distinguished guests, arranged formal dinners and garden parties and had to keep in close touch with the palace. I had many good friends on His Highness's staff. My chief contacts were a Muslim nobleman, the Nawab Khusru Jang, from the state of Hyderabad in the south of India, and Sirdar Nitchan Chand, the Controller of His Highness's guest houses. The latter had started his adult life as a *sowar* (trooper) in my regiment. He came of a distinguished family, was well educated and, when the regiment arrived in Sialkot, he had quarters in the mess compound and supervised the officers' mess as mess *duffadar*. Living with him was his sister, a very lovely Hindu lady of the Dogra race, who was to be partly responsible for the colourful ceremonies I was obliged to attend that summer as personal assistant to the British Resident.

The Maharaja of Kashmir had been married twice; unfortunately neither of his wives had been able to present him with a son and heir. However, it was considered unlucky to marry for a third time, so when he wanted a third wife His Highness was married to a tree. Immediately divorced from his wooden bride, he sent his agents off to search for wife number four – and the search ended in the mess compound of the 6th Duke of Connaught's Own Lancers. The lady in question was the sister of Sirdar Nitchan Chand, our mess *duffadar* in Sialkot. Not only did she have the right blood lines but her horoscope was auspicious; and she had the added distinction of being a real beauty. The Maharaja promptly wed her and our mess *duffadar* was translated into a state official of Kashmir.

In due course the lady did her duty and, in early 1931, in a hospital in the South of France, she produced a baby son. It was the arrival of this heir apparent to the throne of Kashmir that was the occasion of all the festivities that summer.

By the time Her Highness and the son and heir returned from Europe that summer, all the preparations had been made – for their arrival, for the naming ceremony, for receptions, garden parties and banquets. It had taken months of planning, in which I had played my part; but in this time I also came to know a little of the place and its customs.

Srinagar, the capital, lies in the centre of a flat saucer of land, the Vale of Kashmir, surrounded on all sides by the huge bastions of the Himalayas.

72

Bisected by the broad, fast-flowing Jhelum river, with surburbs built largely on waterways linking a series of large lotus-covered lakes, Srinagar has rightly been named the Venice of the East. Dominating the city is a steep conical hill capped by the medieval fort of Hari Parbat. The fort had little military value in the 1930s and was garrisoned by ceremonial troops; from its battlements the guns fired only ceremonial salutes.

The number of guns fired on the arrival or departure of a distinguished guest had great political and social significance, both in Kashmir and in the other states of India. The Government of India published an official list of who was entitled to these 'permanent salutes' and when:

Ruling princes and chiefs and others in India, and certain personages in the Aden Protectorate and in the Persian Gulf are entitled to the following salutes on arrival at, or departure from, a military station, or when attending a state ceremony.

For example, the Maharaja of Kashmir was entitled to a salute of twenty-one guns. Then there were tables of 'personal salutes' and 'local salutes', in addition to which a ruling prince might authorize local salutes for any of his vassals. In Kashmir the Maharaja had two such vassals, the Raja of Poonch and the Raja of Cheneni. These gentlemen were not ruling princes but rather *zemindars*, large landowners. Within the confines of the states of Jammu and Kashmir both were accorded the courtesy of a salute of three guns by the Maharaja, though the courtesy was strictly personal and local; these salutes were not recognized by the Government of India.

One of the most beautiful spots of this lovely city lay at the northern end of the Dal lake: the exquisite gardens of Shalimar Bagh, made famous by the Victorian poem 'Pale hands I loved beside the Shalimar'. The gardens were built on a hillside, falling in a series of formal terraces towards the lake. Close-shaven lawns and exotic flowerbeds were divided by geometrically precise waterways and fountains. Climbing up the terraces one encountered a pavilion on each, until the topmost terrace where stood the house once inhabited by the Emperor Jehangir and his love, Nurjihan, 'Light of the Harem'.

The great day finally arrived early in the summer of 1931. Her Highness and the baby son were arriving. In those days there was no airfield at Srinagar; indeed, within British India there was no air traffic other than spasmodic flights by a few squadrons of the Royal Air Force. Her Highness entered the state by road, via the Barnihal Pass; the rest of her journey was to be by river.

First there was an elaborate reception to greet Her Highness on the riverside a few miles outside the capital. After the inevitable salutes and fanfares, the entire party then joined the river procession, including the Resident, Colonel Ogilvie and myself, embarking in a series of ceremonial barges bedecked with multicoloured flags and flowers and propelled by vast numbers of oarsmen. As we made our stately progress towards Srinagar, past thousands of Kashmiris lining the banks and filling the balconies of the houses, dutifully shouting and waving flags, I was reminded of stories I had read of riverborne processions made by Tudor monarchs on the waters of Father Thames. I am sure the Kashmiri procession was just as spectacular.

In the leading barge were His Highness and his lady. At the reception when I was presented to her I was struck by her pallor and the tremble in her fingers. She looked beautiful, dressed in a superb sari with gold embroidery, but apprehensive. The Maharaja himself was richly caparisoned in tight-fitting silk pyjamas, brocaded jacket and a huge maroon turban; as he moved his outfit glittered with a thousand priceless gems.

The river procession wound its way into the centre of the city and halted at the Old Palace for the naming ceremony. His Highness no longer lived here but it held long and sentimental associations for his family. Besides, the time and place of the ceremony had been decreed by the priests after a study of the baby's horoscope.

It was the first really old Indian palace I had ever visited and I wasn't very impressed. It seemed to be a warren of tiny rooms with poky windows. The main room was jam-packed with people squatting on the floor and chanting and droning mantras. The air became filled with clouds of incense and smoke from ceremonial braziers, and it was very warm. Although I was wearing hot-weather dress of gabardine jacket and drill breeches, I found my crossbelt and the weight of my sword oppressive – and my long Maxwell boots were not designed for squatting! I was much relieved when the naming ceremony ended, late in the evening, and we piled into cars and departed for a well-earned *chota peg* at the Residency.

But that was just the first of the ceremonies; a whole week of receptions and parties was to follow. The majority were all-male affairs; even when ladies were invited they were usually few in number and mostly European. Protocol was all-important, of course: the lesser fry had to appear first, then the more elevated, until finally His Highness arrived with his personal staff and made a grand entrance with a fanfare.

The final and most lavish of the many banquets was held in the Shalimar Bagh. All afternoon and early evening the streams of guests arrived at the gardens by boat or carriage. A few bigwigs came in their automobiles, but in the early 1930s there were not many privately owned cars in the Vale of Kashmir. As darkness fell the gardens took on an enchanted look, with myriad lanterns and small oil lamps flickering from every crevice and along the tops and edges of walls and buildings. In the main building the chief guests gathered round a lavishly stocked bar, while long damask-covered tables, loaded with silver and gold trophies, awaited the diners.

Leaving our car at the gateway the Resident and I made the long walk to the dinner house. I had never seen the gardens so lovely and I must say I was reluctant to hurry through this candlelit wonderland. Colonel Ogilvie, as Resident and thus representing the Viceroy of India, was resplendent in the white mess dress of the Indian Political Department. I duly followed him, a few steps to the rear, in the red, blue and gold mess kit of my Regiment. On reaching the house at the top of the gardens we were ceremoniously welcomed by the Prime Minister of Kashmir and prepared ourselves to wait for the Maharaja. Shortly we heard the band of the palace guards strike up the state's national anthem and the various guards along the pathways were called to attention.

His Highness was a most imposing sight. His jacket was a mass of gold embroidery, emblazoned with the stars and medals of his principal orders, and his legs were encased in tight-fitting white jodhpurs, terminating in gold-encrusted Indian shoes. His saffron turban was voluminous, yards and yards of the finest silk, and sparkling above his forehead reposed the largest diamond I have ever seen outside the Jewel House at the Tower of London.

As the Maharaja entered the hall, his subjects all pressed their hands together, raised them to their forehead and then reached towards his feet in obeisance. The foreigners were presented, bowed and were privileged to shake hands. While His Highness put a courteous face on these proceedings, I noticed that he seemed rather irritable; indeed, he was somewhat short with several of his courtiers. Something had upset him. When everyone had been presented he gazed around the hall in an imperious manner. Suddenly he barked: 'Where's Poonch?'

All the guests gaped at one another but there was no sign of the Raja of Poonch, one of the Maharaja's two senior vassals whose presence at such an occasion was naturally required by protocol. Consternation was on every face. Eventually an embarrassed official stuttered: 'He's not here, Your Highness.'

'Well, find him!' snapped the Maharaja.

Just as two nervous aides-de-camp trotted off to do his bidding, scampering down through the formal gardens to the main gate, clutching their bumping swords by the scabbard, the errant Raja appeared. He obviously knew he had offended. He came running towards us up the terraces pursued by his personal aides. His turban was askew and, by the time he made a breathless and shambling obeisance before his liege lord, he was ashen-faced and shaking with apprehension. After prostrating himself and clutching at His Highness's foot, he blurted out some sort of incoherent excuse. From his Highness's expression the explanation cut no ice.

The Maharaja summoned his Prime Minister and retired to a side room for an immediate cabinet meeting. All of us not directly involved in this pseudo-drama called for another drink to cloak our embarrassment. The atmosphere was uncomfortable to say the least. My boss, Colonel Ogilvie, was like a cat on hot bricks; as British Resident he feared he might be dragged into the affair. He suspected the Maharaja of planning retaliation against the Raja of Poonch, and this might involve the Government of India which would in turn involve him. But he was an honoured guest at the banquet; he could not simply shrug his shoulders and leave the situation to resolve itself.

Suddenly the Prime Minister summoned Colonel Ogilvie and myself to attend the Maharaja. We filed into the side room and found his Highness spluttering with rage. The Raja of Poonch had deliberately insulted him, he said, so he was deposing him! He would announce this at a durbar to be arranged the following day and in the meantime would consider who to appoint as the Raja's successor. This was his decision, which the Resident might now convey to the Viceroy.

The Maharaja had no authority to depose anyone, but Colonel Ogilvie had many years' experience in the Political Department and knew this was no time to argue. He bowed gracefully and told His Highness that he would advise the Viceroy and the Government of India of his decision.

The banquet was then resumed. All adjourned to the hall and a semblance of normality returned. The feast was splendid, but the after-dinner entertainment was curtailed and the Maharaja left early. As soon as he had gone I summoned the Resident's car and returned with Colonel Ogilvie to the Residency. Out came the code books and a lengthy report was telegraphed 'top priority' to Delhi.

At 10 am the following morning we received an official reply from the Government of India, which stated merely that the Maharaja's intentions were unconstitutional, as we knew, and that if he went ahead the Government of India would take certain actions to demonstrate its displeasure. The durbar was scheduled to take place at the palace at 12 noon. We had less than two hours to convey the official warning to His Highness and persuade him to change his mind. A quick phone call to the palace, then off we sped to confront the irate ruler.

On this occasion I had to wait in an anteroom while Colonel Ogilvie had a private audience with the Maharaja; however, my boss soon told me what had passed between them. It appeared that with the coming of morning His Highness's choler had cooled and he realized he had overstepped his powers; but he was still extremely annoyed with the Raja of Poonch.

Colonel Ogilvie discussed with him the various constitutional measures he might use, but none would satisfy His Highness. It looked like an impasse. Suddenly His Highness remembered the gun salutes that he personally had granted the Raja of Poonch, to mark his status in Kashmir. He now decided that this privilege should be withdrawn; the Raja of Poonch would thus return home in disgrace without a gun salute to mark his departure. Delightedly Colonel Ogilvie agreed that this was the Maharaja's right and assured him that the Government of India would raise no objection. The matter was resolved.

The disgraced Raja was to leave Srinagar the following morning. But if we expected him to sneak away entirely without attention, we were mistaken. As the Raja of Poonch in his battered Chevrolet passed beneath the battlements of Hari Parbat fort, the state flag over the main bastion was lowered to half-mast and the smallest saluting gun emitted a puff of black smoke with a noise the equivalent of a very small fart!

So ended the Shalimar Bagh scandal. I stayed on in Kashmir for a few months more, pursuing my duties as personal assistant to the British Resident and enjoying the up-country life to the full. But my position was only temporary, of course, and by the autumn of 1931 I had rejoined the 6th Lancers in Sialkot.

12

The Hog-Hunter's Song

Over the valley and over the level
Through the dark jungle you ride like the devil.
With a *nullah* in front and a boar as well,
Sit down in your saddle and ride like hell!

In the late 1930s I was seconded to the Army Remount Department and
spent several happy and instructive years breeding, buying and raising
horses for the Government. In 1939 I was transferred to the Saharanpur
Remount Depot. This was in pig country, not far from the greatest of all
hog-hunting areas in India: Meerut, in the United Provinces, some forty
miles north-east of Delhi. At Meerut was held the Grand National of the
hog-hunter's year – the Kadir Cup. I knew little enough about hog-hunting
but I did know that you had to be a pig-sticker of some repute, with a stable
of fearless horses, to have your entry for the Kadir Cup accepted. This was
not a distinction I ever achieved.

Hog-hunting was a popular sport in the subcontinent in those days, but it
was most enthusiastically pursued at Meerut, Muttra and Delhi. Generally
speaking, only the male pig was considered eligible for the hunter's spear.
The wild boar of India can weigh well over three hundred pounds; he has
razor-sharp tushes about six inches long, is incredibly speedy and agile, and
knows no fear. Even the lordly tiger in his own jungle will turn away from a
big tusker on the rampage. A quick flick of that massive head with its
wicked curved tushes and man, horse or tiger lies bleeding and dis-
embowelled in a pool of blood and guts. There is no second best for 'Mr

Booker', as the boar is known to his hunter; it's all or nothing. Added to this he has natural cunning and can outsmart the smartest.

This was the character that we sought with horse and hog spear. Cunning had to be matched with cunning and guts with guts. No one in their right mind would go out to hunt the wild boar alone. The hunt was carefully organized. Depending on the number of hunters, heats (or sections) of three or four were formed; when a rideable boar was sighted the nearest heat pursued him and the others waited for the next rideable quarry to appear. A 'rideable' hog was determined by size and sex; immature males and sows were usually excused.

Once a heat started to ride a boar it was full speed ahead. You did not 'ride-off' or interfere with another rider. Unless you rode at full gallop you would soon lose the quarry and your companions also. The object was to get to grips with the pig before the others; however the fight might go, the first hunter to blood his spear in the quarry was considered the winner and could claim the boar's tushes. This claim was valid no matter how long the hunt, nor however many spear thrusts by others in the heat might be needed to dispatch the pig.

The hunter wore his oldest clothes because careering at full gallop through low brush and thorn bushes could play hell with boots and breeches; Moreover, spills were frequent and hunting often took place when the temperature was well over 100°F. A thickly quilted topi which also did duty as a crash helmet, was de rigueur but the most important part of the hog-hunter's equipment was his spear.

Although the shaft of the spear was made of male bamboo, like the trooper's lance, the hog spear was much shorter, only about five to six feet. The butt was a large ball of lead and the point of balance was usually only about ten to twelve inches above the butt; this was where the hunter grasped the spear, rather than in the centre as with the cavalry lance. The use of the two weapons was quite different: instead of meeting your opponent head on, as in the cavalry, in hog-hunting you attempted to spear the pig behind the shoulder as you overtook him. A head-to-head meeting was to be avoided if at all possible! The point of the spear came in a variety of forms, but all were cherished by their owners and honed to a sharpness only surpassed by Salahuddin's scimitar.

Like all great sports where the quarry has some chance of winning, there were certain conventions to be observed; the most important one decreed that a severely wounded boar should never be left without the *coup de grâce*, lest it die a lingering death unwarranted by its gallantry. Besides, it might still have strength enough to attack some unsuspecting woodcutter. But rules and conventions are one thing; interpretation is quite another.

I arrived at the Saharanpur Remount Depot by car, having driven down from the north, and as I was unloading the car my new CO spotted the two hog spears stashed in the back.

'Ah,' he said, 'a hog-hunter, I see.'

But I wasn't, I told him, and explained that I had bought the spears on spec and had no idea of their quality. I had never taken part in a hog hunt. My diffidence was of no avail. The CO insisted that I should join the hog hunt arranged for the following Sunday. Fortunately he did see fit to mention some of the do's and don'ts of pig-sticking, so I had at least a vague idea of how to proceed.

That Sunday morning at about 4 am, while it was still dark, I was awakened by my bearer with the inevitable '*Char, sahib*' (Tea, sir). The *char* was hot and sweet, much as the day promised to be. After a quick wash and shave I donned my breeches and boots and walked out on to the open veranda for breakfast – *chota hazri*. This consisted of more sweet tea, two soft-boiled eggs and the inevitable banana without which in his tummy no *pukka sahib* could properly face the rigours of another day. As soon as I had convinced Adalat Khan, my bearer, that I was sufficiently fortified, I left my bungalow and walked down the driveway to the stables.

The *syce* (groom) was waiting for me, holding the horse I had chosen to be my number one mount for the day's sport, a bay gelding with black points. Known in the horsey world as a Waler and destined for the cavalry, he had been imported from Australia; naturally I named him Sydney. Like many Walers he was no beauty; he had a fiddle head and his back was slightly too long. However, he had a big alert eye, greath depth through the girth and a finely sloping shoulder; he was also fast, with plenty of stamina, and feared neither man nor beast.

Sher Khan, my orderly, was busy wiping down Sydney's already glossy coat. Sher Khan was to ride my second horse, a black Indian-bred from the Punjab, and would carry my spare spear; he was instructed to be ready to hand it to me quickly should I need it during the course of the hunt. A third horse, one of my polo ponies in fact, would be ridden by one of my *syces* who would simply act as horse holder if we should remount at any time. After a quick check of saddles, bridles and spears we mounted and moved off to a prearranged rendezvous within the depot, with the other hunters or 'spears' as they were called. On this particular morning we were organized into two heats, three spears in each. With me in my heat was a visitor from Dehra Dun, Oz Lovett, an officer of the 2nd Gurkhas and a pig-sticker of experience. The third man was Sergeant Haines of the Royal Artillery, a great horseman but like myself a newcomer to hog-hunting.

Roy Mathews, the depot commander, called a conference before we left. As we stood listening to him, leaning upon our spears, the depot's field workers padded silently past on their way to work; in the pre-dawn half-light they might have been ghosts. Our first draw, Roy announced, was to be through the *jhow* (tall grass) on the west bank of the river, and we would start in the small wooded jungle called Ghora Bagh. A number of sizeable boar lay up there during the day and Roy told us they would probably break for the big jungle, Bhansi Bagh, where we had a good chance of catching one in the open. He concluded with a warning to those of us who'd never hunted boar before.

'Mr Booker is dangerous at all times,' he said. 'See you don't get your horse cut – and keep an eye on any pig you wound. I don't want any of my farm hands cut up by a wounded boar.'

With his words ringing in our ears we rode off towards the riverbank, following a long line of beaters beating tom-toms, tin cans and rattles. Among our number was the assistant surgeon with his first aid box; somewhat ominous, I thought. Nearby I noticed a horse ambulance and its attendant veterinary chap, swishing away the early morning flies with his fly whisk. Later we would be followed by the ladies, who planned to join us after sun-up; they would bring the usual necessities of life – iced beer and other cold drinks.

We had reached the *jhow*, ten feet high and very dense. The beaters rattled their drums and tom-toms, shouting and leaping in the air. At any minute I expected to hear a cry of '*Soor!*' (Pig). Suddenly it came: '*Soor, sahib!*' There was a crashing of undergrowth. The pig was just behind me. Sydney pricked his ears and I gripped my spear more tightly. But it was a false alarm; just an old sow high-tailing it out of danger. I watched her trotting off with five *bachas* (piglets) squealing behind her.

A few minutes went by. We rode on through the grass which seemed to be getting even thicker. Then a terrific commotion started to my right, and I heard Oz Lovett shouting. I wheeled around and set out at full gallop in the direction of his call. How Sydney knew what he was doing beats me, but every now and then I felt him rise as he cleared some unseen obstacle. We reached a clearing in the *jhow* and I saw Oz going like the hounds of hell towards the river. As I closed on him I caught sight of a huge boar just ahead of the rider and horse. There was a sudden splash and a column of water rose in the air. Master pig knew his river and had hit the ford.

Oz was close behind the quarry and his horse was gaining rapidly on the pig in the shallow water. I pulled up; it was Oz's pig now. Just as Mr Booker was scrambling up the further bank, the expertly wielded spear took him behind the shoulder. Over he rolled. A few more struggles and a second thrust entered his heart. It was all over. Even to my inexperienced eyes it was a very accomplished piece of spearmanship, and I wondered if I could be as quick if ever I got a chance.

As we went back through the high cover I became separated from my companions. I was trying to get my direction when, with a snort and a crash, a vast black boar hurled himself across my bows. I was after him like a flash. At first I felt selfish satisfaction that the others did not know I was onto a pig; I imagined myself announcing on my return that I had killed a monster all by myself. He certainly was a whopper; he looked much bigger than Oz's pig and had a superb pair of tushes. In fact, I found out later, he weighed more than three hundred pounds. At that time, I weighed one hundred and forty pounds.

At first the pace was slowish. He led me a jinking, twisting route, trying to throw me off his line and attempting to get me to fall into every type of obstacle in that very tricky bit of river bed. I pressed him as close as I could but despite Sydney's efforts we made up little ground in the first half-mile. By then I was well and truly separated from the others of my heat and also from Sher Khan. The sun was up and I was sweating freely, but every time I glimpsed my quarry he was galloping strongly. Gradually I realized his plan. It was to get between me and the haven of Ghora Bagh. I pressed on hard and had nearly reached him when he disappeared into the jungle. What to do? Even if the brush had been less thick, it was useless to follow him in. Within five seconds he might have doubled back and I would have lost him.

Slowly I rode around the outskirts of the jungle, looking all the time for some sign of my quarry. For want of a better plan I decided to ride around the far side onto the open ground between Ghora and Bhansi Bagh. I was some three hundred yards out, facing back toward Ghora, when to my surprise I saw my piggy friend peering out of the undergrowth. Something inside had disturbed him and he had decided to go for the deeper cover two miles away. At this moment he saw me, too. Recognition was instant. He was furious. His big ears flapped in irritation and his little piggy eyes burned bright red. A stamp of the foot, two sharp snorts and out he shot. In a split second I realized he was heading straight for me. What the hell was this? I knew that a cornered pig would charge and was highly dangerous, but I had never heard of a boar deliberately charging a mounted horseman in the open. I hesitated for an instant, wondering what to do. Stay still and meet the charging beast on the spear point? But supposing Sydney lost his nerve at the last moment and spun around? It could be the last moment for both of us. Or did I in my turn charge straight towards my adversary so that we met one another at a combined speed of some seventy to eighty miles per hour? The shock could lift me bodily out of the saddle.

When in doubt I have always believed that the best form of defence is attack. Clapping spurs to the gallant Sydney, away we went in a cloud of dust straight toward the charging pig. I had not noticed that the ground thereabouts was pockmarked with large rodent holes; even if I had, it would have made no difference to my resolve. I crouched low over the saddle, leaning out to my right so that my spearhead was free and pointing directly at the oncoming pig. I just had time to decide where on his body I would aim when we were upon each other.

A more experienced lancer would have aimed low and probably taken him in the chest. In my excitement I aimed for the withers where you normally aimed when approaching from the rear of the animal. At that speed it is difficult to hit a small mark – I missed by inches and slashed him sharply across the rump. He gave a squeal of fury, slashed at my horse's legs in passing and rushed ahead. To save his person poor Sydney performed a twist in the air which would not have disgraced a ballet dancer. Unfortunately, on landing, his forefoot entered one of the potholes and down we came like a ton of bricks.

Luckily we were unhurt and our opponent was going too hard to bother about attacking us on the ground. While we recovered, time was passing and our quarry was making progress toward sanctuary. Our mishap had been witnessed by some labourers in the fields and the news was being shouted back by relay to my friends. Sher Khan was the nearest and started galloping toward the scene with my spare spear. I remounted and the chase began afresh. Master pig had a long lead and I doubted whether I could catch him before he reached safety.

At any rate, I sat down and rode. Sydney was a little winded, but I felt him take a couple of deep breaths and start to stretch into a full gallop. Gradually we began to close. About half a mile from the woods I got a good view of the cut on master pig's bottom; it was not deep but was spurting some blood. Soon I was close enough to see the long coarse hairs on his shoulders and I aimed my spear at this spot. Alas for cause and effect. Master pig must have been hunted before and had another trick up his sleeve. As I dropped the point of my spear towards his back, he jinked sharply across my horse's forelegs with the intention of bringing us down. As he pulled across Sydney's forelegs, I missed his withers and stabbed him firmly far back in the loins. This brought us all crashing down for the second time. However, I knew I must not let go of the spear, so held on like grim death.

My secondhand spear must have been rotten. There was a sickening crunch and the spear broke in two, leaving about three feet of the sharp end thrust through the hog's body, with a similar amount of the bulbous weighted end in my hand. All three of us scrambled to our feet at the same time, all thoroughly shaken. Sydney trotted away with his reins dangling, and the boar and I faced one another. Although badly hurt, he was still full of fight. He snorted and glared at me with his little red eyes. I prepared myself to receive the charge, resolved to bash his head with the leaden butt

83

of the broken spear. My chances would have been nil, but I was determined to give him a run for his money.

Right at this moment I heard the thunder of galloping hooves behind me. It was Sher Khan coming to my rescue. Mr Booker heard the hoof-beats as soon as I did. He was in no shape to take on yet another adversary and safety was only some twenty yards away. With an angry shake of his head and a last defiant grunt, he turned and ran at a steady trot into the undergrowth, the broken spear sticking from his side. I cut short Sher Khan's inquiries after my health and told him to catch Sydney and give me my spare spear. Implanted firmly in my head was Roy's admonition about wounded pigs. But in my inexperience I hadn't understood how rash it was to pursue a wounded boar while it was still comparatively fresh, particularly when one was on one's own. I was determined to kill that *soor ka bacha*, I told Sher Khan, and rode off into the jungle.

The *bagh* was intersected with rides (tracks), some of them familiar to me though I'd never ventured off into the undergrowth before. It was thicker and more tangled than I realized. As I searched I found that Sydney proved more of a hindrance than a help; I kept getting caught in the trailing vines and branches overhead. Deciding that visibility would be better if I dismounted, I slipped from the saddle, looped the reins over a convenient branch and left Sydney while I continued my search on foot.

It did not take long to trace my adversary. He had sought refuge beneath a large tree whose branches trailed to the ground. He was standing with his back to the tree trunk, some fifteen feet from me. As I brushed aside the screen of branches I saw him glaring at me ferociously; yet I still had no concept of what a big angry boar could do. He proceeded to show me – a lesson I am unlikely to forget.

For a second or two he pawed the ground with one forefoot, raising a small dust storm. Then like a flash he was hurtling towards me. I barely had time to drop on one knee and present my spearhead to his onrushing body. The spear took him slap in the chest, but the impact was such that it drove me backwards some five or six yards outside the sweep of branches. Here in the semi-open we fought.

I kept a firm grip on the spear shaft, thrusting it ever more deeply into his body. On his part he seemed to be eager to accept the cold steel. To my astonishment he started to climb up the shaft to get at me with his razor-sharp tushes; he was making the fiercest noises and his efforts shook me like a terrier shakes a rat. I could do little but hang on, kicking him in the face. I was tiring rapidly but I knew that if I let go for a second he would tear me to ribbons.

At that moment I heard Haines's voice calling my name. Summoning the last of my energy I yelled back to him for help. I heard him crashing through the brush towards me. Suddenly he appeared to my right, sitting atop his horse and looking stunned. Indeed, the sight that met his eyes must have been a bloody one. Both the pig and I were bleeding and covered in dust, my face was cut, I had lost my topi and was dancing round like a dervish in my efforts to ward off the threatening tushes. I can hardly blame Haines for being surprised. But a moment later he leapt from his horse and joined in with a will, thrusting his spear repeatedly into the pig's chest, six or seven times. Finally Mr Booker succumbed.

Between us Haines and I managed to drag the dead boar off through the undergrowth. We staggered out of the *bagh* to find the rest of the hunt congregated at the spot where I had left Sher Khan; it seemed he had told them what had happened. Everyone crowded round assessing the old tusker; the experts judged his weight at over three hundred pounds and rated his tusks among the largest and sharpest they had ever seen. I felt rather smug – but Roy Mathews soon disillusioned me. I was a 'bloody fool', he said; not only could I have got myself killed, but Haines as well.

'Above all,' he concluded icily, 'a government horse could have been seriously injured through your foolhardiness!'

I had learned my lesson.

That was in 1939. There was more blood-letting to follow, and on a far more savage scale, as the Second World War began.

13

Journey's End

It was in the winter of 1944. The 6th Lancers were part of the 8th Indian Division in Italy, and I was with them. The Regiment had already seen active service in the Middle East; now we were in Europe. Strictly speaking we were no longer 'lancers' for in 1940 we had been re-equipped and reorganized to meet the needs of modern warfare. But the 6th Lancers we remained, a newly mechanized and light armoured regiment, and as such we played a by no means negligible part in the war.

At the beginning of the war the first divisional commander of the 8th Indian was C. O. Harvey, the very man who had recommended that I join the Bengal Lancers; by now he was a general. The divisional arm flash was a form of General Harvey's personal crest: a bunch of cornflowers over the motto *Carpe Diem*. Later the division was taken over by General 'Pasha' Russell, who commanded it during the great battles in Italy. He it was who modified the original arm flash; the cornflowers became clover leaves, their stems entwined to form the letters 'I' for India and 'V' for Victory, the 'I' crowned with a lucky four-leafed clover and the 'V' with two three-leafed clovers. So was born the 'Clover Division' (and after the war the division's reunion association was called the Clover Club; long may it thrive!).

That winter of 1944 we were in the higher country of the Apennines, north of Florence and practically overlooking the plains of northern Italy. The weather was a mixture of snow alternating with icy rain and it was bitterly cold. I was commanding 'A' Squadron of the 6th Lancers. We had just been dismounted to take over a sector of the infantry line from the Rifle Brigade, and the centre of our defensive area was to be Monte Moro.

Like many of my men, I dare say, I felt this was neither the place nor the weather to be fighting on foot. We were cavalry, after all; besides, I just don't like walking. And I think there was an element of romance in it too: riding a good horse straight at the enemy or even driving in an armoured car or tank. Obviously the horse or tank could not prevent you being blown to bits, but to me it seemed better than ending up a mangled mess in some stinking trench. In any event, I was firmly convinced that I would not be killed in action. This is not to say I never felt frightened; who hasn't? Only those who lack all feeling or sensibility. And there was many a frightening moment to come.

The day we took over from the Rifle Brigade, I went for a daylight reconnaissance of the lower slopes of Monte Moro, along with my four troop leaders – all Indian warrant officers. We kept a wary eye on the crest of the mountain where the Germans had located their gunposts; should any of them open fire we were ready to jump for cover. There was a certain amount of long-range shelling and other noises, but we seemed safe enough.

It was *Risaldar* Hari Singh, my senior troop leader, who drew my attention to the high-flying fighters in the sky. There they were, with the red and blue roundels of the RAF, cruising overhead like a security blanket: four Spitfires of the Desert Air Force. It was a reassuring sight, for the Germans would never open up on us while the RAF was there.

Suddenly we heard the whine of aircraft descending at speed. I glanced aloft and could hardly believe my eyes. The Spitfires were peeling off, one after another, and diving straight for us. The whole world seemed to explode as cannon shells burst around us. We scattered and took what cover we could. It was all over in seconds. There were only two minor wounds among the five of us, but it was an inauspicious start to our spell on Monte Moro.

Our orders were to hold the line from a series of fortified farmhouses and outlying posts and to indulge in some aggressive patrolling, if possible to capture some prisoners for identification purposes. The day we moved into our new positions I received a reinforcement officer. He was not a 6th Lancer but had been posted to us from another cavalry regiment; aged about twenty, he had come straight from officers' training school and had not yet heard a shot fired in anger. He seemed quite a pleasant young man, but he struck me as a somewhat nervous type. I decided to put him in the Rifle Troop.

At the time, the lancer squadrons of the regiment were organized into four troops with a small squadron headquarters. Three of the troops, in their normal role, fought in armoured cars, three cars per troop with four men in each. Dismounted, they comprised a very small posse. The fourth troop was the Rifle Troop, which usually rode in armoured half-track vehicles and comprised about forty men in all; they were therefore our strongest element for the type of job we now faced. The second-in-command of my Rifle Troop was a very experienced and much decorated Indian warrant officer. I informed him that the new British officer would take over command of the troop but that he should keep an eye on the newcomer and generally teach him the ropes.

I had a quiet chat with the young officer, welcoming him to our regiment and telling him the form. then I called in the second-in-command and briefed both men on a mission I wanted Rifle Troop to undertake that night. From our positions I pointed out a small copse about half a mile up Monte Moro, where we believed the Germans posted a listening party every night; it would be the Rifle Troop's job to infiltrate the German position, collect at least one prisoner or corpse, then get back off the exposed hillside as soon as possible. After some discussion they worked out a plan of attack that I approved and at about 2 am that night I watched them filing silently up the hill.

The night was dark and stormy and filled with the usual far-off noises of battle: the occasional crump of shells, the chatter of machine guns. But the men of the Rifle Troop were seasoned soldiers and I anticipated no trouble. I returned to my farmhouse HQ to snatch an hour's sleep. I had no sooner dropped off than a deafening crash awoke me. Running out of the house, I could hear the thunder of a full-scale fire-fight. It was coming from the hillside: long bursts from Bren guns, bursting grenades, staccato bursts from Browning and Sten machine pistols. Ye gods, I thought, they must have run slap-bang into a German fighting patrol.

I called up the armoured car troops and we all stood to. The noises were coming closer; we could hear people running and shouting. Suddenly there appeared a wild mud-covered figure running down the hill towards us. It was my new troop leader. He had lost his helmet and was firing his Sten gun at random. Behind him appeared half a dozen men from Rifle Troop, looking confused and anxious.

Grabbing the young officer's Sten, I pushed him somewhat roughly into the farmhouse and tried to find out what had caused the rout, why he had abandoned the remainder of the troop on the hill. But he was almost incoherent, babbling about a heavy attack by hundreds of Germans. I told him to stay put while I returned to the trenches where the rest of my men were standing to.

Gradually the Rifle Troop trickled back down the hill and gathered in bewildered groups. At first I could only make out that there had been a lot of firing and the Lieutenant Sahib had kept shouting 'Bhago, bhago!' (Run, run!). The troopers hadn't known what was going on, so they obeyed his orders and ran. Finally a small party arrived back, carrying a wounded man; one of their number was a very irate Indian warrant officer and he it was who explained what had happened.

It seemed that as the troop moved up a pathway in the darkness, one of the men had stepped on a *schuh* mine, a lethal German mine in a wooden casing and therefore difficult to detect. There was a loud explosion as it went off right in the middle of the troop. The lieutenant thought the Germans were attacking and opened fire; the noise, of course, attracted the enemy's attention and the whole hillside erupted in a noisy and spectacular firework display. The young officer lost his nerve and shouted to the men to run; but most of them stood firm, only moving back when ordered to do so by their Indian officer.

Looking round at my men's faces, I realized the squadron was in danger of a serious breakdown in morale. Something had to be done about the lieutenant. I returned to the farmhouse and found the young man sprawled at the table with his hands over his head. I had seen men before who succumbed to their feelings in the stress of action. In the First World War they called it 'shell-shock'; in this war it was called 'battle fatigue'. Whatever its name, such behaviour was understandable in men who had been under extreme tension for long periods of time, but I could not accept such an excuse for a man who ran away the very first time he heard a bang in the night.

I jerked the lieutenant to his feet and asked him his version of the story. It was totally different, of course; he claimed they had been ambushed by the Germans and the troop overrun. He admitted that he had shouted *'Bhago, bhago'* but said he had only done so to extricate as many men as possible, intending to reform the troop lower down the hill. After some probing on my part, however, he finally admitted the truth. The exploding mine, so close to him in the darkness, had panicked him.

All right, I thought, everybody gets frightened at times; everybody is allowed one mistake. But this mistake had to be put right, for the sake of the squadron's morale. I told the lieutenant that after a suitable interval he would have to go back up the hill. When the men had had a chance to recover their breath, when the Germans might be expected to have gone back to sleep, I wanted Rifle Troop to retrace their route up the hillside – though not to look for prisoners this time; that would have been too ambitious.

'You'll just take a quiet disciplined walk up to the spot where the incident occurred,' I told him, 'and see if there's any of our equipment still lying about. If so, you'll collect it and return to base. Is that clear?'

The young lieutenant just looked at me.

'It's quite simple,' I said. 'Any questions?'

'No, sir,' he said, 'but I'm not going back up there in the dark for anything.'

Journey's End. My thoughts suddenly went back to that night in London when I'd gone to the theatre before leaving for India. Here was I in an almost identical situation to that of the company commander in the play: confronting a subordinate who refused point-blank to obey orders. Yet I could hardly emulate my counterpart in the play and pull a pistol on this young man, to threaten him to obey 'or else'. That would be pure melodrama – and in reality I knew it would result in my facing a court of enquiry. Besides, the lieutenant looked so frightened.

I turned my thoughts to possible alternatives. Then I remembered that time-honoured cure of the British Army, for times when the weather was particularly bad or the fighting very tough – the issue of a good dollop of excellent Jamaica rum. I called my batman and told him to fetch a couple of bottles of rum from the quartermaster *duffadar*, then to brew up a can of 'gunfire'. 'Gunfire is the Indian soldier's traditional brew of tea – strong and customarily drunk with Nestlé's thick condensed milk, it would put heart into a louse; laced with a generous dose of rum it is formidable.

As my Irish grandmother always said, 'There are more ways of removing a man's boots than by hitting him over the head with a shillelagh.' Figuratively speaking, I started to remove the young man's boots. A few mugs of the potion coupled with a lot of quiet talking finally got him to his feet, a little unsteady, to be sure, but ready to go. Another slug of rum and off he went. Mission accomplished, next morning he left on the visiting ration truck.

So much for my version of *Journey's End.*

Within a few days 'A' Squadron's aggressive patrolling had forced the enemy to withdraw, and we moved in to occupy his vacated positions atop Monte Moro. The Germans' new positions, on a hill to the north, lay across a col from us in the centre of which stood a little church; we had been told that an enemy patrol used it as an observation post. I was now planning to lay an ambush at the church.

Corps Intelligence had received information that the Germans we were facing, the 3rd Parachute Division, had been replaced by an infantry division. The word trickled down to me with orders to confirm this. I was told to get the necessary identification – meaning prisoners. So once again I got the Rifle Troop together. We had not yet received a replacement for the young British lieutenant, and though the Indian second-in-command was more than competent, I decided to go along too.

Together we laid our plans. The Indian officer would go to the west side of the church with the bulk of the troop while I would take three men and edge round to the east, where we believed an enemy sentry was posted; with luck, I hoped, we would be able to take him prisoner. Our planning was hampered by the fact that we hadn't had a chance to reconnoitre the col and we'd only been able to scan the church through binoculars; we had a good view of the west side but the ground to the east was obscured. Another frustration was the weather – snow, sleet and mud would make the going very difficult. I would have preferred to postpone the raid, but the orders from above were urgent.

We set off in a snowstorm which gradually turned to sleet. It lashed down, half blinding us, but at least it covered our approach. We reached the church and the party split. I led my three men round to the right, or east, and as we skirted the church, edging along with the wall to my left, I realized that the ground here fell away in a steep slope.

Our information was that the enemy patrol usually came down to the church just before dawn. Tonight they were there ahead of us. I saw a figure about five paces ahead, threw up my pistol and fired. As I did so, I started to slide down the icy slope, followed by bursts from the German's submachine gun. The leading trooper, managing to keep his feet, flung a grenade at the sentry, but, while I continued to slither helplessly down the hillside, the German raced back round the church to rejoin his fellows. He ran slap into a fire-fight with the rest of Rifle Troop.

Fortunately for us, on this particular night the enemy had sent out only a small spotting patrol, whereas we were a full-strength fighting patrol. The fight was of short duration. Most of the Germans withdrew, but my men caught two as they tried to leave the church through a back door. When I eventually managed to scramble back up the slope, the troopers were already shouting to me that the show was over.

Identification of the two Germans showed that they belonged to the 3rd Parachute Division. Our Corps Intelligence had been misinformed; the German formation had not been relieved by infantry. A few days later we were withdrawn and moved to another part of the front. But I was to remember this small incident long after the war was over.

I was back in India and, having resigned my commission, was by now in business in Bombay. One Sunday I was invited to lunch with an Indian friend at his Juhu beachhouse. My friend had recently opened a factory to manufacture nuts and bolts in collaboration with a German firm, so on my arrival at the beachhouse I was not surprised to be introduced to another of his guests, a German by the name of Friedrich Koch.

'He had quite a distinguished career in the Germany army,' my host told me, and added laughingly, 'Perhaps you might have faced each other some time!'

We started to compare notes; I asked him his unit; he asked me mine.

'The 8th Indian Division?' he exclaimed. 'Oh yes, I remember you. Your arm flash was a sort of yellow flower design on a red ground.'

He wasn't far wrong, I told him, because the clover design on our arm flash was indeed yellow on a red background. We chattered on about times and places long past and both agreed that the winter of 1944 had been particularly unpleasant; I suppose that was how Monte Moro got into the conversation.

Friedrich Koch was the German sentry I had fired at beside the church below Monte Moro. On that occasion we had tried to kill each other – and here we were, eight years later, reminiscing over a dry martini on a beach in India! Such is the futility of war, mellowed sometimes by the chance meeting of former enemies. A year or so later I was passing through Düsseldorf and called Herr Koch from the airport. He came to see me and I still cherish the very attractive picnic set he gave me as a memento and a reminder of our first meeting.

1. The author at Miri Khel Camp, October, 1930.

2. The Khyber Pass, looking towards Peshawar.

3. Ali Masjid Gorge, Khyber Pass.

4. Patrol of the 6th Lancers on the Kajauri Plain, October, 1930

5. The river procession for the naming ceremony of the heir to the Maharaja of Kashmir, River Jhelum, Srinagar, 1931.

6. The Resident and the author arriving for the naming ceremony.

7. (*Above*) Officers of the 6th D.C.O. Lancers, Lahore, 1932. The author is third from left in the front row.

8. (*Below*) H.E. The Governor of the Punjab's camel carriage arriving at Lahore Racecourse, Governor's Cup Day, 1934.

9. The author when commanding the bodyguard to H.E. the Governor of the Punjab, Governor's Cup Day, 1934.

10. Men of 8th Indian Division storming the Irmgard Line, Italy, April, 1945.

11. Staff Officers of the Pakistan Military Academy, 1948.

12. The author when Commandant of the Pakistan Military Academy, Kakul.

13. General Sir Douglas Gracey, Field-Marshal Sir Claude Auchinleck and Brigadier Francis Ingall.

14. Liaquat Ali Khan, Prime Minister of Pakistan, before presenting colours to the Cadet Battalion, Pakistan Military Academy, 1948.

15. Pakistan Military Academy Polo Team, Abbottabad, 1949. The author is on the left.

16. Miss Fatima Jinnah, sister of Mohammed Ali Jinnah, visiting the Pakistan Military Academy, 1949.

17. Visit of the President of Pakistan, Khawaja Nazimuddin, to the Pakistan Military Academy. On his right is General Sir Douglas Gracey, on his left the author.

18. Visit of Liaquat Ali Khan, Prime Minister of Pakistan to the Pakistan Military Academy, 1949.

19. Brigadier F. H. B. Ingall, DSO, OBE, late of 6th Duke of Connaught's Own Lancers, and Mrs Ingall, St George's Day Ball, 1962.

14

Chasing Chickens

The war wasn't over yet, however. The 6th Lancers spent that winter of 1944–45 in Italy and by February, 1945, we found ourselves across the Apennines in the vineyards north of Ravenna, in the plains of Lombardy.

This was a low-lying area and two rivers, the Senio and Santerno, flowed through the vineyards some three miles apart. Narrow and not very deep, the rivers were contained by levees or floodbanks about thirty-five feet above the surrounding countryside, steep and insurmountable for any vehicle or tank. In fact the Germans had made them still more impregnable; the Todt workers, the German labour organization, had tunnelled, revetted and reinforced the banks with concrete. Moreover, the area was pock-marked by the enemy's anti-tank weapon pits and machine-gun posts. Yet this was the terrain over which we would have to attack.

Within this area a narrow strip was held by the cavalry units of the British 2nd Armoured Brigade, all of us in a dismounted role to give the infantry a chance to rest and train for the forthcoming spring offensive. The 6th Lancers, under command of the 2nd Armoured, had fought through the German lines and now were located in fortified farmhouses surrounded by barbed wire and minefields. In places we were less than a hundred yards from the German positions, which overlooked our own. We engaged in furious grenade battles, usually at night, each side lobbing missiles at the unseen opponent. Occasionally they sent barrels of explosives rolling down a bank towards us, fitted with time fuses set with ingenious cunning. We had a preponderance of artillery and kept up a continuous barrage; the Germans, for their part, used their *nebelwerfers* and rockets to damaging effect. The *nebelwerfers'* characteristic wailing noise was nerve-sapping in itself and a direct strike by one rocket could demolish a large stone farmhouse.

It was therefore a rather unpleasant week or two for those of us engaged in this period of static fighting. It did, however, allow us an opportunity to gather detailed knowledge of the enemy's strength and dispositions. Towards the end of February we were relieved of our infantry role and withdrawn to a training area. All ranks were looking forward to a mounted role again and the possibility of a breakout.

The training lasted a month, as we practised for the long-predicted spring assault. The 6th Lancers – as part of the 8th Indian Division, itself a part of the British V Corps – would have to prepare for our forthcoming movements on this difficult terrain.

Divisional HQ arranged for me to fly over the enemy positions on the Rivers Senio and Santerno – the Irmgard Line, as the Germans called this defensive line in the Po Valley. I wasn't too sure what I had let myself in for and my few illusions were dispelled when I went to meet my pilot, a major in the Royal Artillery; he led me to an artillery spotter plane, an impossibly fragile-looking Gypsy Moth.

The major laughed at my expression and explained that the Germans would never fire on us for fear we would direct our own artillery on them.

'But some dumb Kraut might just decide to let loose with his Spandau,' I objected, adding, 'I want a steel helmet.'

He looked at me as if he'd finally decided all cavalrymen were nuts. 'What the hell will you do with a steel helmet?'

'Sit on it,' I replied, and we both burst out laughing.

We had a fascinating hour cruising over the carefully camouflaged German positions and I got a very good idea of the terrain over and beyond the front lines. Alternately studying my maps and the real topography below me, I began to grasp the enormity of the task that faced us. Broken as it was by innumerable canals and ditches, this was not the most suitable ground for the 6th Lancers' light armoured cars.

Made by General Motors, our 6-wheeled armoured cars were usually very reliable vehicles for cross-country jaunts, but there are limits even to what a tracked vehicle can do. So we practised for days in our cars, trying to tackle the hazards I now knew we would meet. Sometimes we deliberately ditched a car to see how to get it out again. It wasn't easy. Then one day I had a minor brainwave. During an earlier tour of duty in the Middle East we'd had many a tussle with sand, and the engineers had come up with a device which I suspected might prove equally useful here. I took myself off to the main engineer park south of Ravenna and there found just what I wanted: eighteen-foot sand channels of reinforced steel.

Below the revolving turret our armoured cars had a wide sloping side panel, at either end of which the engineers welded a strong hook; for transportation purposes the channels were suspended from these hooks, hanging free but secure. In the Desert we had often run into soft sand, but by removing these channels and laying them over the sand we had found that the cars were able to get across. Now the channels would be used to help us cross marshy ground and levees.

I soon got the divisional heavy repair shop to weld the hooks on our cars and we hung the channels from them. My idea was that, when one of our troops of three cars came to an obstacle where the channel could assist them, one crew would remove the channels from the other two cars while they in turn covered the operation with machine-gun and cannon fire. And in the event the channels did come in very useful.

Spring had come to the Po Valley. The weather was fine and the big assault was imminent. The German forces were tasting the bitterness of defeat all over Europe, but on the Irmgard Line they still held strong. The date of the assault was finally decided: 9 April, 1945.

The British V Corps was initially going to attack the River Senio from two sides: the 8th Indian Division on the right and the New Zealand Division on the left, bypassing the town of Lugo. General Russell, in command of the 8th, decided to attack on a narrow front with four battalions of two of his brigades in the leading wave. As soon as the infantry was across the river, the engineers were to blow gaps in both levees and drop into the water one or two specially adapted Sherman tanks, which had trackways welded to their superstructure in place of turret and gun. These would form the foundation for an assault bridge over which the 6th Lancers would cross, to protect the right flank of infantry brigades advancing on the second objective, the River Santerno.

Opposing V Corps was the full-strength LXXVI Panzer Corps of the Tenth Germany Army. The 8th Indian would face three enemy divisions: the 98th Infantry, 362nd Infantry and 42nd Jaeger Divisions. In reserve they had the 29th and 90th Panzer Grenadiers, and also, far to the north, protecting the entrance to the Brenner Pass, the elite 1st Parachute Division.

With such a concentration of the enemy within the area, our most vital weapon would be the element of surprise. For weeks before the attack Allied forces made continuous feints and diversions to deceive the enemy over our intentions. Security was tight and every tank, gun and trench was camouflaged. But we also had impressive support, including two hundred and fifty fighter bombers and five hundred heavy bombers of the US Air Force – and, a recent addition to our forces, the Italian Cremona Division.

This regular unit of the Italian Army had opted to join the Allies after their country's surrender. Obviously, as secrecy of our plans was all-important, they were not to be briefed until after our troops were committed; then they would be ordered to stage a feint attack on another sector.

If all went according to plan, once through the German defence positions of the Irmgard Line the 6th Lancers had to punch a hole in the Argenta Gap. Lying south of the large city of Ferrara, this feature was a bottleneck, a potential obstacle to any large-scale troop movements to the north; with marshy areas to the west and a large lake to the east, the main north-south *autostrada* and other ancillary roads ran through the Gap. It had to be secured if we were to exploit the breaking of resistance on the Irmgard Line.

The attack was launched in the early afternoon of 9 April. The five hundred Flying Fortresses came in at 20,000 feet on a prearranged bearing from the Adriatic. Their object was to lay a carpet of bombs over the first obstacle, the River Senio. To guide them to the right river our own light anti-aircraft batteries exploded a continuous line of air-burst shells at 18,000 feet just on our side of the river. It all went like clockwork. While the Flying Fortresses released their bombs in a thunderous deluge over the German lines, our artillery pulverized the floodbanks and the area immediately beyond.

The shelling lasted four hours. The noise was shattering and one doubted whether any living thing would be in a position to resist when it ceased. And more was to come: the fighter bombers now stormed in to strafe the German positions. Meanwhile the infantry started to push forward and with them went a concentration of flame-throwers. Watching from a few hundred yards back I saw the gouts of flame belching across the vineyards, consuming all in their path. Smoke and flame rose into the air; it seemed to me that our infantry must be consumed also. Now that the Germans could pinpoint the actual place of the attack, they erupted in savage retaliation, pounding our own lives with their artillery, mortars and *nebelwerfers*.

The battle went on all night. The Todt lines were well prepared and the defenders were there and ready when our infantry finally climbed the levees. The two sides now engaged in fierce hand-to-hand fighting. By morning, however, our leading battalions had secured the River Senio. It had been the most difficult obstacle the division had encountered in two years of war in Italy. Losses had been heavy on both sides. Two Indian soldiers of our Division won the Victoria Cross for their actions that night.

By first light the following morning four cableways had been erected over the Senio and anti-tank guns and jeeps were being slung across. By mid-morning the bridge mounted on sunken Sherman tanks was ready. This was our cue. But with so many units and such limited access to the bridge, progress was slow. We came under heavy shell-fire from the

Germans' 88mm guns. By noon, however, I had got my HQ across, followed by the Regimental Gun Troop French 75ms, mounted on half-track weapon carriers, whom I sent on to deploy their guns in an orchard some few hundred yards from the bridge; they would protect our right flank while I got the rest of the regiment across the river.

I was standing on the engine louvres of my armoured car, watching the Gun Troop's progress, when it happened. The Flying Fortresses arrived overhead, hundreds of them moving in a stately parade towards their next bombing target, the River Santerno. Behind me the bridge was coming under fire from the Germans, but in the midst of the cacophony I suddenly heard a new sound: quite different from the thunder of guns, it was like a downpour of rain pattering on fallen dry leaves. I looked up. There were the heavy bombers flying straight and serene towards the Santerno – but between them and me the sky was full of falling 'daisy-cutters'. These are 40lb anti-personnel bombs which explode on impact leaving practically no crater, – but lethal to anyone not under cover.

'*Down!*' I yelled at the Gun Troop and crashed head-first into the open turret of my car, nearly breaking the adjutant's neck.

Of course, the men hadn't heard me. None of them had chanced to look up and presumably hadn't realized what the strange noise was. This tragic accident cost us dearly. The Gun Troop was completely out of action. Out of forty there were twenty casualties and all the guns had been hit. Among the dead were two of my officers and several good NCOs were severely wounded.

I did not find out until later, but our rear echelons also caught it, just as they were approaching the bridge to cross. Lieutenant August Ricciardi, our Italian liaison officer and a staunch believer in the Allied cause, had been badly wounded – as had Balwant Singh. Singh had been our mess wine steward and had served the 6th Lancers faithfully for twenty years; at the outbreak of war he had volunteered for the Indian General Service Corps so that he could stay with the regiment and look after the creature comforts of his sahibs.

The Gun Troop were mainly Muslims and high-caste Hindus and I now faced an interesting but sad religious problem. The Muslim dead, I knew, had to be buried with their faces towards Mecca, but the Hindus were another matter. In the Imperial Indian Army all religious beliefs and customs were sacrosanct, and I wanted to be sure I did the right thing. Burial of the dead was not a task that would normally have fallen to me. Usually in battle there is a flow of casualties from front to rear, but here we were isolated, with little hope of evacuating our casualties for at least twenty-four hours. It was a warm spring day and I could not just leave our comrades where they had fallen.

I decided to ask my senior Indian officer, the Regimental *Risaldar* Major, who was a Hindu. He was at his post in the rear echelon, so I called him on the radio to ask for his advice.

He did not hesitate. 'They should be buried temporarily, Colonel Sahib,' he told me. 'If you have any cord or string, set it alight and clasp the dead man's right hand around it before you bury him. If you have no cord, use a lighted cigarette.'

And so we did.

We finally crossed the River Santerno, mopping up the area to the north and west. Throughout northern Italy the enemy resistance was weakening but there were still pockets of strong opposition. Just south of the Argenta Gap the 8th Indian Division halted to reorganize. This area was being cleared by two other divisions from V Corps, the 56th and 78th, and the 6th Lancers assisted them through the Gap. The bottleneck was behind us at last and now we moved on towards Ferrara.

In the countryside south of Ferrara there was heavy fighting and the regiment was in the forefront. Then on 21 April the 8th Indian passed through the 56th and 78th Divisions with orders to take Ferrara and attempt a crossing of the River Po. The 6th Lancers now reverted to the 8th Indian Division command.

The enemy was determined to stop us crossing the Po and to deny us the city of Ferrara. To this end he committed a part of the 26th Panzer Division which had suffered little and still had all its tanks and equipment. The 6th Lancers tangled with their Royal Tiger tanks south of the city and on the airport. We lost a number of cars, but kept these monsters busy while General Russell outflanked the enemy positions and seized the city. Unfortunately most of the heavy tanks got away in the night, crossing the last bridge over the River Po and then destroying it.

By now all organized enemy resistance south of the river had ceased. The V Corps Commander decided to keep the enemy on the run and ordered General Russell to cross the Po on 24 April. This was not to be. The Po presented a problem quite different from those other rivers, the Senio and Santerno. The Po was two hundred yards across with a fast-flowing current, and all the bridges had been destroyed. None of our bridging equipment was suitable so we had to send for special pontoons and ferries; this was going to delay us for at least two days. But our divisional engineers refused to be beaten by any river, however wide and fast. They fabricated a sturdy Class 9 raft and by the night of the 25th we were starting to cross.

It was a dizzy experience. Driving the heavy cars on to the raft was a juggling act in itself and the navigation on the rafts would have given a Hooghly River pilot apoplexy. At each corner of the raft was an outboard motor manned by a sapper and the speed of all four was co-ordinated by an officer with a whistle. Talk about a one-man band: we whirled round and round on the water until, finally, when he played the correct tune, we made it across and landed on the far bank. All this was accompanied by artillery and machine-gun fire from the enemy. It says much for the harassing fire from our side that we lost no men or vehicles in the River Po.

The bulk of the enemy had retired beyond the River Adige, some fifteen miles north of our crossing point on the Po. However, there were many strong rearguard parties protecting the main routes north. The 6th Lancers' 'C' Squadron and RHQ had landed near Occhiobello and, as soon as we had all regrouped, the party moved about half a mile inland for a brief break of hot tea and hard rations before moving on. Everyone was pretty tired as it had taken eight hours in the darkness to ferry us all over the river. Refreshed, the squadron and RHQ started to thrust northwards. By the afternoon *Jemadar* Fazal Dad's troop of armoured cars had reached the substantial wooden bridge over the Canale Bianco. This was the only bridge in the divisional line of advance that the enemy had not blown up. It seems that the German sappers had run out of explosives, so they set it on fire. When the troop appeared on the scene, the centre span was burning fiercely. The cars got themselves into hull-down positions, with just their turrets showing above ground, and opened fire on the German defences across the Canale. Meanwhile, under cover of machine-gun and mortar fire the troop extinguished the blaze. The bridge had been taken intact.

I heard the news on my radio and raced to the spot, knowing this would greatly facilitate the division's move to the north. The gap in the bridge planking where the fire had been fiercest was only about ten foot across; so, while other elements of the squadron shelled and machine-gunned the further bank, we hauled two of the sand channels – still slung on the side panels of each car – onto the centre of the bridge. To my delight they were long enough; the first car crept across slowly but safely. That was that. The whole of 'C' Squadron passed over and mopped up the defenders. The channels remained in position for several days until the engineers were able to repair the bridge; the rest of the 6th Lancers and 17th Infantry Brigade, as well as many other divisional units, crossed over them. The fitting of those channels to the cars had certainly paid a good dividend.

Once past this obstacle we encountered little opposition until we reached the River Adige. Here Corps halted our advance while they sorted out the many units converging for the final *coup de grâce*. The River Adige was not such a formidable hurdle as the Po; it was swift-running but only a hundred and fifty yards across, with steep banks suitable for Bailey bridging. Division decided to push one brigade across to form a bridgehead so that a Bailey could be launched.

On 28 April General Russell asked Corps if he might send the 19th Infantry Brigade and the 6th Lancers across the Adige to take Venice. In the event, V Corps decided that only the 6th Lancers should be sent on this Venetian odyssey. I was delighted – and determined to deal the staggering Wehrmacht a final smashing blow.

Between us and Venice stood Padua and our old enemies, the 26th Panzer Division, as well as units of three other German divisions. But disorganization had set in; I felt that if I could hit them at high speed from several directions at once, we might punch a hole through their defences and find ourselves in Venice by nightfall.

I held a coference with my squadron commanders and told them I would have no administrative 'tail'; our striking force would comprise only the armoured cars of each squadron plus the Rifle Troop's scout cars filled with extra ammunition and petrol. The men of the Rifle Troop would stay by the Adige, there being no room for them in the scout cars. RHQ would have three jeeps, one containing a special long-range radio provided by Division; they had given me three coded report lines. I had decided to launch my three squadrons on parallel roads with RHQ following the centre squadron and I would endeavour to keep control from there. If any squadron ran into serious opposition I would send support from one side or other. But cars that were hit would be left, and casualties also. We would take no prisoners. Speed was to be the maximum possible.

We crossed the Adige at 0905 hours and were off, the three squadrons up to three miles apart as we sped northwards. On every side there was confusion: enemy units firing on one another and the dreaded 88s spinning on their mountings, firing armour-piercing and high-explosive shells in every direction, vainly trying to hit our speeding cars. It was exhilarating. In the occasional lull in the firing one could hear the powerful V8 engines of the cars screaming as at times they hit sixty or seventy miles an hour. It was just like three foxes chasing chickens in a hen run.

Dutifully I made my first two report lines in code. Then as we neared Padua I threw caution to the winds. We had done fifty miles in two hours. I called Division.

'I'm within sight of Padua and am swinging right onto the Venice *autostrada*,' I announced.

'Congratulations!' replied the GSO1 of the 8th Division, Ian Chauvel. 'But hold it a minute . . .'

He explained that there was a big row on at Corps HQ. General Harding wanted us to stop so that the New Zealanders could go through and enter Venice first.

I was outraged. I was not under General Harding's command, but Corps

100

HQ could certainly stop me. I thought quickly; I was damned if the 6th Lancers and the 8th Indian Division would be done out of a little final bit of glory – and all for the sake of inter-division politics. The New Zealanders were a super division and General Freyberg, their commander, was one of the famous soldiers of the century. But I felt Venice was ours; it was in our sector and I didn't want to give it up.

I asked Ian where I could contact General Harding; he was with General Freyberg somewhere on the western outskirts of Padua, Ian replied.

'Go to it,' he added. 'But don't upset the Big Sunrays!'

'A' Squadron was in the process of swinging east on to the *autostrada*. I called their CO and explained the problem, suggesting that he get all his cars off the *autostrada* and on to secondary roads; if he received orders from General Harding's HQ to stop, he should ignore them and press on to Mestre, the roadhead for Venice. The rest of the regiment I halted just south-east of Padua while I went off in my jeep in search of the 'Big Sunrays' – our codeword for commanders.

I found their HQ about noon and a staff officer escorted me to General Harding's caravan. His face was red and furious. The 6th Lancers were right off course, he snapped; we should be back on the River Adige. And he ordered me to get my squadrons off the *autostrada* at once. Playing for time, I told him I'd been given explicit instructions by V Corps to go to Venice and that we had left the Adige at 9 am that morning.

He looked at me in disbelief. 'Good God, you must have been moving like the devil!'

He sent for his Brigadier General Staff and ordered him to get General Keightley, the V Corps Commander, on the radio. I was sent outside to wait. There was another small delay; I hoped 'A' Squadron was making progress. But minutes later I was sent for again, and heard the sad tidings. General Keightley had ordered me to withdraw my regiment from the *autostrada* and leave the route clear for the New Zealand Division. I could not disobey. I called my leading squadrons on General Harding's radio and passed on the new orders. I shook hands with the General and made my departure.

'A' Squadron had not made the progress I had hoped for, being considerably delayed on the secondary roads. However, just short of Mestre, Squadron HQ and one troop of 6th Lancer cars were lined up alongside the *autostrada* – cheering ironically as the New Zealanders passed through to take Venice.

We all knew the real glory was ours, but it was a disappointing end to our thrilling chase across the plains of Lombardy.

15

'Quit India!'

Even before the outbreak of the Second World War it had been obvious that India was divided over her future. Political agitation and clashes between religious groups had already indicated that India's status in the British Empire was changing. Indeed, the Empire itself was changing; that much was clear to me by the time I returned to India after the war.

By 1947 I had been appointed one of the three senior General Staff Officers (GSO1) in the Military Operations Directorate at Army Headquarters, New Delhi. This was considered a plum job; occupants of the position were vulgarly referred to as the 'heaven-born', meaning that one's feet were firmly on the ladder to preferment; with any luck one would rise to the rank of general and might conceivably end up as Commander-in-Chief. Or so it had been in the piping days of peace; but 1947 was to be the year of Partition.

As GSO1s we three were to have a major role to play in the partition of the armed forces, but initially our prime duty lay in maintaining internal security. This entailed the allocation and despatch of troops to help the civil authorities wherever and whenever communal violence broke out. By 1947 these clashes were an almost everyday occurrence: Sikhs attacking Muslims, Muslims attacking Hindus, and vice versa. With few exceptions, the only troops upon whom we could call were from the comparatively small number of British battalions still serving in India, or from the famous fighting divisions of the Imperial Indian Army, recently returned from foreign service.

Being composite in nature, these Indian Army divisions comprised mixed units of Muslims, Sikhs and Hindus, as well as representatives from the many other races and religions in this vast subcontinent. Yet now they were called upon to face riots being instigated by their co-religionists, whether Muslim, Sikh or Hindu. Such was their esprit de corps, however, that they behaved with perfect discipline and restraint right up until the moment of Partition, when they were divided into separate units for transfer to either Pakistan or India.

As I was in charge of the section dealing with internal security, my principal involvement was in the trouble spots. I was therefore under no illusions about the latent hostility that continually threatened to break out into open violence. Partition was clearly the only answer: two separate states, Pakistan and India, one Muslim and one Hindu. But like Lord Wavell, the Viceroy, I believed that the only way to achieve this bisecting of the continent was for the transition to take place slowly, methodically, policed throughout by a strong and impartial military force; the alternative would be a bloodbath. I believe Lord Wavell's suggested time-scale for the transfer of population and division of assets was five years. But the British Government under Mr Attlee, then Prime Minister, had already decided that India should be granted independence by 1948 – and Lord Mountbatten agreed. Attlee sacked Wavell and appointed Mountbatten instead.

So Mountbatten arrived in India as Viceroy in 1947. To give him his due, I believe his original intention was to try to persuade the Muslim League to cease agitating for partition. Had he succeeded, a cohesive India might have become independent within the time specified. But to anyone who knew India this was clearly a pipedream. Mr Jinnah, President of the Muslim League, was adamant that his people should no longer be subjected to what he described as 'domination by the Hindu majority'; he insisted on nothing less than a separate state.

The Congress Party, meanwhile, under the leadership of Nehru, was encouraging civil disobedience in pursuit of independence. After six years of war their patience had run out. As the 'Quit India' campaign gathered steam there was an atmosphere of 'Let's do it quick!' Between them, Nehru and Jinnah applied such pressure to Mountbatten that he had to cave in. India would be partitioned within a matter of months, and achieve independence the following year.

I happened to find myself very much at the hub of things, both because of where I worked and because of where I lived. Serving as I did on the General Staff of Army Headquarters, my office was situated in a big sandstone block on the south of Kingsway, that majestic driveway designed by Lutyens to sweep down from the portals of the Viceroy's residence. I was thus close to the offices of the Chief of the General Staff and even the Commander-in-Chief himself.

Not only that, I lived on the Viceroy's estate. I was staying in the house of an old friend, Colonel Douglas Currie and his family. Douglas Currie had been Military Secretary to Lord Wavell; now he fulfilled the same role for Lord Mountbatten. As the Viceroy's senior military staff officer, all matters military that concerned the Viceroy had to pass through his office, as well as a multitude of administrative affairs pertaining to the Viceroy's staff and movements.

As a resident of the estate I was privileged to use the facilities: private golfcourse, squash courts, swimming pool, etc. While doing so I often met not only the staff but the Viceroy himself on an informal basis. As any student of British social customs will know, 'shop' – meaning business – is rarely discussed at a social gathering. However, in 1947 the pot was boiling fiercely and a final date for partition was on everybody's mind. For some that date would spell the end of a career; for others transfer to the British Army; a transfer from the Indian Civil Service to the Foreign or Colonial Service; a period of service with the new India or Pakistan; or just plain retirement to the Cotswolds. As the hot weather of 1947 wore on, people became increasingly edgy, speculating with ever more urgency about the future. So the subject of the Partition date came more and more to everyone's lips, even over a chota peg at the club. There was one occasion when 'shop' was discussed at the dinner table and, being outspoken, I put my foot where I should have put my grilled chicken.

It must have been some time in July. The date for Partition had just been announced – 15 August. Douglas Currie and his family had arranged a small, private dinner party for the Mountbattens and a few members of the staff, and they very kindly included me. I had had a hectic day at Army Headquarters, parcelling out exhausted soldiers to deal with the increasingly frequent outbreaks of communal violence. The situation was deteriorating daily and I was very troubled; a party would provide some welcome relief.

It was a very hot night and dinner was to be served on the lawn behind the Curries' house, but first we gathered for drinks in the drawing-room. Conversation during cocktails was inconsequential and Lord and Lady Mountbatten were as charming as usual. The Curries' butler appeared and announced: 'Khana tiyar, hazoor.' So we all trooped outside to the spotless dinner table laid out with silver and crystal that glittered in the garden lights. The summer evening was full of the usual Indian hot-weather sounds: the croaking of innumerable bull frogs, the occasional screech of a nightjar or the hoot of an owl.

We started with iced consommé, well laced with sherry, then the entrée was just being served when the inevitable subject was raised – the imminence of Partition.

'It all seems so sudden . . .' someone remarked.

There was a silence; everyone was waiting for the Viceroy's reaction. Lord Mountbatten smoothly agreed that it was perhaps rather 'sudden' but went on to say that in his experience that was the best way to get things done.

'You give your staff a plan,' he said, 'and ask how long they need to put the plan into operation. Let us say they estimate four weeks. Then you tell them, "Do it in two!" Everyone is shocked into action and you surprise your enemy.'

Whereupon Ingall's voice was heard to say, 'And who is your enemy, sir?'

I realized I had made a gaffe. On the other hand, Mountbatten's attitude had strengthened my view that the Viceroy, and therefore London, still did not really understand India or the Indians. The 'enemy' indeed!

I know it would have engendered anti-British sentiment but I am still convinced that it would have been far better for India if Lord Wavell's long-term scheme had been adopted. Where his plan might have cost hundreds of lives, the Attlee–Mountbatten plan cost, I estimate, around half a million.

So India was to become independent. My Army, the Imperial Indian Army, would no longer exist. I was still young, only thirty-nine. I had had a successful war. I had achieved my fondest ambition – to command my regiment in battle. In the staff world I had held the most sought-after post of GSO1 of one of the famous fighting divisions, the 8th Indian. I had been decorated. But now what would I do? I felt somewhat confused. While I had a recurring urge to try something new, and was toying with the idea of a business career, it was the desire to remain a soldier that was foremost in my heart.

I could, I knew, transfer to the British Army. All officers of the Indian Army had been graded in the event that they might transfer; if they elected to retire they would receive a bounty; if they chose to transfer the bounty would be smaller. I also knew that certain selected officers might be retained on the Imperial Indian Army List, for temporary secondment to either the new Indian Army or the Pakistan Army in training or advisory capacities. Those taking up such appointments would be paid the higher bounty, and the officers concerned would be carried on a special list at Supreme Army Headquarters, New Delhi, commanded by Field-Marshal Sir Claude Auchinleck; Supreme HQ would continue for at least five years and officers on loan to the two new armies would be permitted to count the time served towards their regular pension.

I had two years to go before qualifying for my full regular pension in the rank of major, my official peacetime rank. Special rules did allow high ranks held during the war to count towards enhanced allowances, but the basic requirement was for a full twenty years' service. It therefore seemed that if I now opted out of the Army, I would forgo a full pension.

It was while I was mulling over the various alternatives that I was summoned to see Sir Claude Auchinleck, the Commander-in-Chief. This was most unusual. Comparatively junior officers are not normally sent for directly by the C-in-C. I made a few enquiries, but no one knew why I'd been sent for: not my immediate boss, the Director of Military Operations, nor even his boss, the Chief of the General Staff. I was still very much in the dark as I straightened my tie, pulled down my jacket and set off to see the big white chief.

I had known Sir Claude Auchinleck throughout my service; although I was to have my differences with him later, I always found him the most charming of men. I was ushered into his office and he immediately put me at my ease. Another man was present, whom I recognized from his photographs in the Press – Liaquat Ali Khan. Liaquat was a lawyer by profession and he was to be the workhorse who put the new state of Pakistan together; he became Pakistan's first Prime Minister. But at the time his presence only served to deepen my mystification.

Minutes later, all was clear. I was being offered the opportunity of a lifetime – the opportunity of founding the Pakistan Military Academy.

16

Partition

Naturally I accepted the invitation to set up the Pakistan Military Academy. As Sir Claude Auchinleck and Liaquat Ali Khan explained, the new Pakistan Army obviously needed its own supply of young officers – and quickly. In short, Pakistan would need a Sandhurst, a West Point, a Duntroon of her own. During the war I had spent a short but successful term as Commandant of the Armoured Corps Officers' Training School at Ahmednagar, near Bombay; I thus had some first-hand knowledge of what this job would entail. The appointment would carry the rank of brigadier to begin with and would last as long as it took to get the place established and producing first-class young officers on a regular basis, though in the first instance I signed an agreement to serve Pakistan for three years, until August, 1950.

Not everyone thought I was doing the right thing. The Adjutant-General, Sir Reginald Savory, told me bluntly that he thought me a fool; he had taken an interest in my career ever since the day he inspected the OTS at Ahmednagar while I was in command. I ought to opt for transfer to the British Army, he said; he even showed me my grade and said that as an officer with 'A1' against my name I would have an excellent future in the British Army. 'Damn few in that bracket,' he barked. 'You'll be a damn fool not to transfer to them.'

But I had made up my mind. I had once hoped I might return to Sandhurst as an instructor; but this was even better. To create a military academy from scratch and command it – I just could not resist.

Time was short, however, and there were innumerable preparations to be made before I could leave Delhi. The whole country seemed to be erupting in violence and I wondered how best I could reach Rawalpindi, a large city in the north of what would be Pakistan, where the Pakistan Army would have its headquarters. Eventually I decided to drive up from Delhi on 14 August, the day before 'P-Day'.

One of my chief worries concerned my old and faithful servant, Adalat Khan. A Muslim, he had been in my employ some ten years; obviously I would take him to Pakistan with me. The roads between Delhi and Rawalpindi were very unsafe, however; every day came news of Muslims being attacked and massacred by Hindus, as well as vice versa. As an Englishman I knew I would probably be safe enough if I ran into an ambush, but if Adalat were with me and we encountered a hostile bunch of Hindus, his safety would be less certain. It seemed a better bet to send him by train; so far they had not been attacked and I had heard that, as so many Muslims would be travelling north to reach Pakistan at Partition, armed escorts would be provided. I booked Adalat on the train to Rawalpindi on the 13th.

The days sped past. While I rushed around completing my arrangements and saying goodbye to everyone in Delhi, Adalat packed up all my gear; by this time I had accumulated rather a lot and it amounted to several boxes full. It was 13 August. I took Adalat to the main Delhi railway station, along with all my belongings. Then we discovered that the special escorts had not yet started on the refugee trains heading for Pakistan. I was not too worried, however; railway passengers were still far less likely to be attacked than travellers on the roads. To be on the safe side I told Adalat to stay on the train no matter what happened; he wasn't to worry about my baggage which would in any case be loaded into the goods van. I bade him farewell, promising to meet him in two or three days at Flashman's Hotel in Rawalpindi. Even I didn't know to what extent we were tempting Fate.

The escorted trains which started a few days later were a disaster. Coming south they were full of Hindu refugees, going north they carried Muslims; either way they were liable to attack by opposing factions. The trains were stormed by hundreds, sometimes thousands, of men, and the small escorts of a dozen or so men were totally inadequate. No one had anticipated the ferocity of these attacks or the careful planning that went into them. Ambushes were laid either in stations or in the open country where the track had been tampered with. The raiders were often armed with mortars and light machine guns, acquired from Assam and the borders of Burma where a mass of redundant weapons had been dumped at the end of the war, buried in huge pits to save transportation costs.

The escorts were invariably swamped by the sheer number of attackers.

In some cases they were worse than useless, particularly if the insurgents were their co-religionists, when they simply stood by and watched the slaughter. There were too few British officers to spare for this duty, but when they were available they often put up a fantastic show. One such escort commander heard, while they were already under way, that the engine crew of his train had been bribed to stop at a prearranged place; an ambush would almost certainly await them. He was in the rear coach and the trains in those days did not have communicating corridors. Nothing daunted, he climbed out on to the roof and staggered forward from coach-top to coach-top, swaying perilously, until he reached the locomotive. The engine driver, guessing his mission, slammed on the brakes; but the officer was not to be denied. He bashed the driver and the fireman with the butt of his pistol, then drove the train through the prospective ambushers at sixty miles an hour!

Alas, many British officers were killed carrying out this sort of duty. There was a party of twenty men of the Queen Victoria's Own Corps of Guides, under one of their own officers, returning from southern India to their home station of Mardan, now in Pakistan. With the exception of the British officer they were all Muslims. Somewhere in central India their train was stopped and attacked by Hindus. Naturally the officer fought alongside his men. It is said they fought until their ammunition ran out, then fought on with their bayonets, but eventually all were overwhelmed by the Hindu mob. Their bodies were never found.

Not content with slaughter, the attackers usually ended by looting the contents of the trains, searching the bodies of their victims for valuables and rifling through boxes of belongings.

But I could only assume that Adalat was safe as I set out on my own journey north on 14 August. Had I waited another week, I am sure I would not have got through in one piece.

The distance from Delhi to Rawalpindi is approximately 500 miles by road. I planned to do it in two stages. First I would drive the two hundred and thirty miles to Jullundur and spend the night there. I hoped to have a chance of meeting an old cavalry officer friend, Brigadier Thyrett-Wheeler, who was in command of a brigade of the Punjab Boundary Force; their HQ was at Jullundur. The next stage would take me across the Beas River and on via Amritsar to the new border and thence to Lahore. Lahore would be the first Pakistani town on my route, and I thought I might spend another night there before pushing on to Rawalpindi.

Early on the morning of 14 August I duly set off in my small black drop-head Vauxhall, with my two Australian terriers in the back. The top was rolled down, my bedding roll and hand luggage were slung in any old how, but on the front seat beside me I placed a .45 Colt automatic. I was wearing uniform, with my black 6th Lancer beret on my head.

The first stage was quite uneventful. I had some sandwiches and beer (very hot by the time I opened it!) and, pausing only for refreshment, made steady progress towards Jullundur. There was much more traffic than usual on the Grand Trunk Road, but I encountered no special cause for delay. Arriving in Jullundur in the late afternoon I found myself a bed at the local *dak* bungalow, a traveller's resthouse, and unloaded my gear from the car, noticing as I did so that one of my tyres looked rather jaded; I thus had to put off my visit to Brigade HQ for a while in order to visit the bazaar and search for a replacement. I was in luck, however, and the problem was soon resolved.

I found Brigadier Thyrett-Wheeler in his office; he was too busy to talk at the time but invited me to dinner that evening. I returned to the *dak* bungalow and took the dogs out for a walk, remarking how peaceful everything seemed in Jullundur, then rejoined my friend for dinner. After an excellent meal and a brandy or two, my host asked where I was heading. Lahore, I told him, then Rawalpindi. His reaction rather startled me.

'Lahore?' he echoed. 'You're mad!'

Tomorrow was Partition Day and anyone crossing the new border would certainly run into trouble, he said; for my own safety I should be travelling with an escort of armed men. I argued, but he was insistent. He arranged for some watchdogs to join me on my departure at 6 am the following morning.

He should have locked me up. By 5 am I had already left – no escort, just me and my two little dogs. I felt I would be much safer on my own.

I already knew that the most dangerous part of my journey would be between the Beas River and the border, thirty miles beyond Amritsar. This was the heart of the Sikh country. I was not surprised, therefore, when nearing the Beas River bridge I had to stop for a wild party of Sikhs, three to four hundred strong, who were streaming across the road towards a nearby village. They looked to me like a real Sikh *jatha*, an organized raiding party; all were armed to the teeth. But a casual glance told them that I was alone and unlikely to interfere with their plans, and I took the precaution of keeping my pistol out of sight. They paid me no attention. They rushed past shouting their war cries: '*Wah, Guru-ji ka Khalsa! Wah, Guru-ji ki fateh!*' (Hail to the Guru of the Sikh religion! Hail to his victory!)

I drove on towards Amristar. The road was now increasingly littered with the pathetic flotsam of a people in flight: shoes, old pots, broken wheels, bits of cloth. And then I started to come upon the bodies. There were scenes of carnage everywhere. In the distance I could see the smoke and flame of innumerable fires, I could hear yelling hordes. Amritsar itself was like the cities I'd seen in Europe in the war, just after the enemy had withdrawn:

burning houses, smashed doors and windows, broken carts, telephone lines down, streets empty. There wasn't a living soul to be seen.

I began to feel I had made a mistake; perhaps my friend in Jullundur had been right. The presence of a company of infantry would undoubtedly have been comforting here. But the Boundary Force could hardly have spared the men; they were already fully stretched as they responded to one call after another, following reports of trouble.

As I left the outskirts of Amritsar I passed through one of the most bestial scenes I have ever witnessed, though it wasn't till later that I heard what had happened. Four or five hundred Powindah nomads had been ambling peacefully along the Grand Trunk Road towards Amritsar, following their usual route. Half the year they wandered through the lower highlands of Afghanistan and surrounding states, but at this time of year they were starting to filter down through the Punjab towards winter grazing for their animals and the cities where they could do some trading. If they had any religion at all it was Islam, but as nomads they were loners, apolitical, non-violent. Near Amritsar this nomadic party was set upon by a *jatha* of Sikhs, hiding under cover of crops and armed with automatics and light mortars. Men, women and babies were all slaughtered, even the goats, donkeys and camels.

It must have happened very shortly before I arrived, for I could hear the survivors being chased through the crops by their killers. It was horrible, like a scene from Dante's *Inferno*. There was nothing I could do; I simply had to keep going. I picked my way through the corpses and was past the worst of the shambles when some of the murderers must have spotted me. They opened fire on the car. I swung onto the dirt berm at the side of the road, confusing any pursuers with a spume of dust as I sped towards the border. Later I stopped to inspect the damage: two bullet holes through one fender. We'd been lucky, I told my two very shaken little dogs.

I crossed the border with no further trouble and drove into Lahore, the capital city of the Punjab, which I had come to know so well while stationed there in the thirties. The outskirts appeared normal. I drove past that bastion of British officialdom, the Punjab Club, and opposite it the Gymkhana Club where I had had such fun at all the dances. Government House seemed just as aloof and austere as I remembered it. But then I entered the Mall with all its European shops and cafés, and the scene began to change. Alongside Queen Victoria's statue stood a Sherman tank, obviously cleared for action. Houses were burning or half-demolished, telephone wires were festooned everywhere, shops had been broken into by looters.

I felt quite sick and disheartened. Where was the wonderful freedom that my people had granted so hastily? Everyone seemed to be grabbing their freedom on the end of a knife or cudgel. I drove to Faletti's Hotel and ordered a drink. Some of the old servants were there, most of them Muslims, and one or two recognized me. All were horrified and apprehensive, despite the fact that they were safely within the confines of their new homeland. I thought of their co-religionists struggling to reach that promised land from the Muslim areas of India.

And there was the other side of the coin: desperate Sikhs and Hindus trying to cross the border in the opposite direction. More than ever now I was convinced that Wavell had been right, Attlee and Mountbatten wrong. As for Sir Cyril Radcliffe, the man whose pencil drew the partition lines on the map, he had done his best; but, with no understanding of India or things Indian, he had made several crass errors. The worst mistake was to allot that predominantly Muslim area, Gurdaspur, to India; the effects of this will be felt for decades, possibly for ever.

I decided not to stay the night in Lahore after all. I finished my drink and started the last leg of my journey. Personally I felt somewhat safer in that I was coming to serve the state of Pakistan. But there were madmen everywhere and one could not relax for a moment. Near Wazirabad there were further signs of recent atrocities: a Muslim mob had stormed a stationary train, looting and murdering the Hindu occupants. Such was the backdrop to the first day of partitioned India.

Late in the evening I drove into the compound of Flashman's Hotel in Rawalpindi. The strange, incomprehensible bush telegraph of the East was still working. I did not have time to walk from my car to the hotel office before Adalat Khan appeared to take charge of my life again. After my hideous journey I was delighted and relieved to see his open, honest face. He greeted me equally warmly, but with an anxious look. I soon discovered why.

Adalat's journey, in fact, had been much less eventful than mine. It later turned out that his had been the last of the refugee trains to cross the border unmolested. A Hindu crew had driven as far as the embryo border, then a Muslim crew had taken over. He had reached Rawalpindi safe and sound.

Not so my luggage. I had not been on Adalat's train – hence his anxious greeting. Wearily I decided that it had probably never even left Delhi and I gave it up for lost.

Weeks later, when I had settled down at Army HQ in Rawalpindi pending selection of a site for the new Academy, a warrant officer walked into my office one morning and told me he had just seen some boxes addressed to me on the platform at Pindi station. I grabbed Adalat and we rushed down to the station. It was there, all of it! I just could not believe it, in view of the daily reports of assaults on trains and the complete looting of their contents. The goods had arrived some six weeks after despatch from Delhi.

It seemed so strange that I instituted enquiries. It turned out that my belongings had been sent on a regular goods train; these trains carried no passengers and were staffed by Hindu crews up to the border, then handed over to Pakistani crews. Supposedly, on the Indian side of the border the locals assumed a goods train was destined for Indian stations, and vice versa on the Pakistan side. And a goods train contained no refugees so it was not considered worthy of an attack!

So I did get my household goods and souvenirs back after all. Indeed, most of them are still in my possession to this day.

17

The Pakistan Military Academy

As soon as I had found myself a quarter at Flashman's Hotel I reported to Army Headquarters. To enable me to draw pay and allowances, I found that I was attached to the General Staff Branch in an appointment similar to the one I had held in Delhi, but it was purely a paper job. At a staff meeting presided over by the Commander-in-Chief, the Chief of the General Staff and the Director of Military Training, I was formally designated Commandant of the embryo Pakistan Military Academy.

I was told that I should plan for an Academy with a battalion consisting of four companies and a curriculum to be spread over two years. It was emphasized that the half-trained cadets coming from the Indian Military Academy must be finished off and commissioned post-haste; these, of course, were Muslim cadets who had opted for Pakistan. The IMA had been in existence since the mid-thirties when Indian gentlemen, desirous of pursuing a military career, were no longer sent to Sandhurst for training but to the IMA at Dehra Dun instead; this was part of the programme to 'Indianize' the Indian Army. During my time at Sandhurst there had been several Indian cadets but they all came from wealthy families, able to pay the rather heavy fees. Dehra Dun offered a comparatively expense-free course, and therefore was able to attract Indian boys from a much wider field. This also was the intention at the PMA, where the cadets would receive modest pay and allowances during training. In fact, any young man with the necessary physique who had a matriculation certificate and was able to pass the interview was adjudged acceptable.

Beyond these basic requirements, however, all was yet to be decided.

114

Because of the hasty creation of this new state of Pakistan, no one had had much time to work out the details of the country's infrastructure, whether at government level or in the military. Everything had to be created anew and in a hurry. It was a massive task, therefore, that faced those of us involved in the decision-making process – sometimes daunting too. But it was a wonderful challenge and the atmosphere was one of determined excitement.

Initially I found myself given a free rein to make what order I could out of the confusion: to find a suitable location for the new Academy, to find the money and the staff as well, and to supervise the decisions relating to the curriculum. None of this was very straightforward, particularly as I had to work through the usual channels of the new Pakistan Army. In fact, my first problem brought me up against all sorts of obstacles: how to finance the Academy.

I began by estimating what staff, premises and equipment would be required, and working out a budget to cover these costs as well as the actual running costs of the place. This in itself was no easy task but finally I had produced the necessary budget. Now I had to persuade the Army to approve my budget and furnish the finance. It was to prove a most exhausting and time-consuming process.

Eventually I had to appear before the Adjutant-General to argue my case. A newly promoted officer, the Pakistani Adjutant-General was extremely pompous and difficult to deal with; he also seemed vague about what was required of him and hesitant about making decisions. The new Army's pay and accounts department proved parsimonious beyond belief and there were times when I was made to feel I was asking for the moon, when all I wanted was the very basic funding their new Academy required.

These early brushes with senior officers of the Army did not make me 'best beloved', but I was determined to forge ahead as fast as possible. At last I had their approval of my budget. Now it was time to tackle the next problem: where should the new Academy be located?

I already had a place in mind. Back in the thirties, when I had married for the first time, my wife and I sometimes rented a house in Abbottabad for the summer. Lying in a valley 4000 feet above sea level, surrounded by the foothills of the Himalayas between northern Pakistan and Kashmir, Abbottabad had its own military cantonment and was not considered a true hill station like Kashmir, Murree or Simla. But summer temperatures were reasonable and the rents were cheap. Besides, Abbottabad had a fair polo ground and the local garrison played polo all year round. I used to send my polo ponies up there at the beginning of the hot weather; my wife, the servants and the ponies stayed for about six months and I usually managed to get two months' leave in July and August when I could join them.

I had thus come to know the area well. For many years Abbottabad cantonment had been the base depot for two regiments of Gurkhas, the 5th Royal Gurkha Rifles and the 6th Gurkha Rifles, as well as the 13th Frontier Force Rifles, a regiment of mountain artillery and a brigade headquarters. Five miles away there had been another cantonment at Kakul, which in the thirties had been home to the Indian Army School of Artillery and more recently, during the Second World War, a training school for young officers of the Royal Indian Army Service Corps (RIASC). The area therefore had all the logistical back-up of a well-established military station – supply depots, engineer services, etc. Moreover, it was only eighty miles from Rawalpindi by road; there was also a rail link from Rawalpindi, though it terminated at Havelian, ten miles short of Abbottabad. Thus the area was within fairly easy reach of Pakistan Army Headquarters in Rawalpindi.

Kakul, as I remembered it, had been small but modern. The houses were built of brick and stone with all modern conveniences: running water, electricity and flush toilets – light years ahead of most military stations in the thirties! During the war the RIASC had expanded even faster than other branches of the Indian Army, and I knew their training facilities had expanded accordingly. I checked with AHQ to see whether Kakul was now occupied. To my delight they told me it wasn't – so I decided to go up there and confirm my feeling that this would be the perfect location for the new Academy.

I drove up the Grand Trunk Road and into the foothills until the road debouched into the broad valley where Abbottabad lay. All around the valley stood the beautiful hills, rising towards the east where the majestic Himalayas wore white ermine capes and conversed with the sky. What a superb backdrop for the Academy! The valley itself was good farming country, green and lush, and the local tribesmen, the Shinwaris, were comparatively law-abiding – compared that is, with the trans-border tribes to the north-west.

Arriving in Abbottabad, I found everyone in the usual state of upheaval caused by Partition. The Gurkhas were leaving – 5RGR destined for the new Indian Army, 6GR to become part of the British Army – and the 12th Frontier Force Regiment was taking their place. But the training school at Kakul was, as I had been assured, empty.

The former facilities of the RIASC were all I had been led to expect. The staff quarters and large staff mess were in tip-top shape. New buildings housed four permanent student messes and single quarters for about four hundred students, married officers' hutments, a large lecture hall plus smaller study halls, two cinemas and much else besides. There were a few shortcomings, but these I felt were outweighed by all the advantages. This was the ideal place for the Academy.

I returned to Rawalpindi and wrote a report recommending that Kakul be the chosen site. I discussed it personally with the Commander-in-Chief, General Sir Douglas Gracey, as well as with the Chief of the General Staff and the Director of Military Training, all of whom were British regular army officers on loan to Pakistan. Kakul's training school was duly chosen to be the site for the Pakistan Military Academy.

There now followed hundreds of meetings at AHQ in Rawalpindi as we began to get down to such matters as staff, courses and equipment. Again I found myself clashing with the gentlemen of the military accounts department over my equipment indents, as well as with several awkward customers who had been newly promoted and wanted to flex their authoritative muscles. However, most Pakistani officers, I am glad to say, realized that the founding of the PMA took priority over all new training establishments except the Staff College at Quetta, and gave me their full support and co-operation.

One man whose support I could always count on was in the Ministry of Defence, and thus one of my ultimate bosses, Iskander Mirza. We had known each other at AHQ in India and were on very good terms. Following several unnecessary delays on the question of staff, I decided to ask Iskander for his help. I wanted his authority to pick any officer I needed, over the head of the Military Secretary at AHQ whose job was to arrange the posting and allocation of all officers throughout the Pakistan Army.

But first, at an interview with Iskander, I explained that I wanted a regimental sergeant-major from the Brigade of Guards in London, plus six Guards drill sergeants. Iskander agreed, and said he would get the Pakistan Government to contact the British. But England, too, was in a state of upheaval after the war, and my requirements could not be met in full. Thanks to Iskander, however, I did get one invaluable man Regimental Sergeant-Major V. C. Duffield MBE of the 3rd Battalion, Coldstream Guards.

Mr Duffield had never served in the East before and knew nothing of Islam or the country in which he was to serve, as I discovered when he and his wife arrived in Pakistan. I did my best to acquaint him with my experience of nearly twenty years in India, describing the current situation in the subcontinent and trying to explain what I thought Pakistan expected of us. An intelligent and receptive man, he quickly saw what an exciting prospect it was for an Englishman to take part in the building of this country's future. Although he and Mrs Duffield had practically no social life in the Academy, and the minimum of creature comforts to which they must have been accustomed, they settled down very quickly and Mr Duffield soon won the respect of all he met. A super drill instructor, he became a legend at Kakul for the high standards of drill, discipline and turn-out he required of the cadets – standards that the Pakistan Army still enjoys.

The other drill staff who came from England were not of the same quality: only two were Guardsmen, while the others came from regiments of the line and did not meet the standards I wanted. Some had personal problems and, after all, had been posted willy-nilly into a foreign country which was still suffering its own birth pangs. Ultimately I sent them all home, and told the indispensable Mr Duffield to build a Pakistani drill staff. This he did with great success, despite his nonexistent Urdu. Much of a drill sergeant's armoury is his ability to castigate his victims verbally; Mr Duffield's demeanour and vocabulary were superb and, after an astonishingly short time, I was amazed to hear his team of Pakistani drill staff using the very same admonitions in Urdu coupled with identical gestures!

As for the other staff, Iskander Mirza was as good as his word; thanks to him and the Prime Minister, Liaquat Ali Khan, who was also Minister of Defence, any officer I asked for was made available and I had soon collected an excellent military staff. All were young – yesterday my colonels were captains and my majors were lieutenants – but most had seen active service in the Second World War. Anything they lacked in experience they made up in unbounded enthusiasm. I could not have found a better or more loyal team.

My first Deputy Commandant and Cadet Battalion Commander was Colonel M. A. Latif Khan, of the Baluch Regiment, who had fought with great gallantry in Burma and had been awarded the Military Cross. When his name was first proposed I had some doubts; it was hinted that his sympathies were anti-British. However, as soon as I met Latif I took an immediate liking to him. At our first interview I discovered that he was intensely nationalistic – in fact, after he left my staff his ambitions would get him into serious trouble. But I asked him point-blank if he was indeed anti-British; if so he would obviously be unsuitable as my deputy. He was very honest and explained that his prejudice was not against the British nation as a whole but one man in particular. It all boiled down to a tactless senior British officer treading on a young and sensitive Latif's toes. He told me frankly that *he* had made enquiries about *me* – and that in his opinion the Government could not have selected a more suitable person than myself to found the Academy! Needless to say, we struck up a lasting friendship.

Another officer I was fortunate enough to obtain for the Academy, in the capactiy of a company commander, was Latif's brother-in-law, Major Abid Bilgrami. These two young men were married to charming and sophisticated sisters from the noble house of Bhopal – all were refugees from India. The ladies were to play a valuable role in organizing the social life at Kakul.

One of the first things that had been decided in our meetings at AHQ had been the length of the course and, in general terms, what subjects would be taught. I obtained the latest curricula from my alma mater, Sandhurst, from West Point in the USA, Duntroon (the Australian Academy) and the Academy in Canada. Roughly speaking, the syllabus was divided into two-thirds academic subjects, one-third military training. We worked day and night, sketching out the syllabus for each subject and writing précis after précis. Suddenly I realized we had reached a stage when the material requirements of many of these subjects were lacking. The military end was fine and growing day by day, but where were the textbooks and lab equipment?

One day I was sitting in my hotel room in Rawalpindi reading the *Civil and Military Gazette*; published in Lahore, this was the most influential newspaper of the Punjab – at the turn of the century its editor was none other than Rudyard Kipling. The leading article caught my eye: it was on the subject of education. The writer was bemoaning the fact that Pakistan had few seats of learning and the best of the colleges, in Lahore and Rawalpindi, were being vandalized and looted by hooligans from the bazaar. He went on to say that all the best Muslim universities were now across the border in India – Osmania, Islamia and Lucknow – but practically all of their leading teachers had emigrated to Pakistan, destitute and without work; no one had any use for them, it seemed.

This article was doubly interesting, for not only did we lack equipment but also instructors to teach the arts, humanities and science. In short, apart from my military staff, I needed academic staff. The Adjutant-General's branch had suggested I call upon the services of the Army Education Corps and I did in fact take on one excellent lieutenant-colonel as Director of Studies, four majors and a number of captains. But I needed many more, and the rest of the AEC's people were in my opinion incapable of teaching the subjects we required. Their main job in peacetime was teaching the common soldier to read and write Urdu in Roman (that is, English) script as opposed to the *shikasta* form; they also taught English to some advanced students, but that was about the limit of their usefulness.

I dropped my paper and headed for the office of the senior civilian administrator, the Commissioner of Rawalpindi. I told him of my plight. I needed textbooks and various sorts of equipment desperately; AHQ had no funds to buy what I wanted – and yet in colleges in Lahore and Rawalpindi these precious assets were being looted and smashed by *goondas*, gangs of organized rioters. The police had their hands full and could not spare the men to stop the rioting. It might be years before Pakistan began producing her own educational material, and certainly before she had the foreign exchange with which to purchase it abroad. But I needed it *now*, I said.

Might I collect a few soldiers and undertake a spot of organized looting myself?

To say the Commissioner was taken aback is an understatement. He was no newly promoted Deputy, but quite a senior member of the old Indian civil service and was accustomed to legal and civil niceties. However, he took my point and finally sent for the Superintendent of Police. We had a short conference and agreed on a time and place for me to launch my looting raid. Next I went to see the Commanding Officer of the Frontier Force Rifles, to borrow the services of his men, and to the local supply officer in Abbottabad who loaned me several three-ton trucks. On the appointed day we duly descended upon the colleges of Rawalpindi and systematically looted all we could cart away. It was exactly what we needed to start our first courses – indeed, I believe that some of our spoils from that day are still in use at the academy.

But I wasn't finished yet. Having acquired my materials, I now needed more staff to instruct my cadets. I went to see the Commander-in-Chief in Rawalpindi – the Adjutant-General, I felt, would probably find my scheme too hard to swallow – and showed him the editorial in the *Civil and Military Gazette* that had motivated me. What I proposed was that we should advertise for civilian professors and lecturers to join the academy – the very people who had fled from India and now found themselves without a job. General Gracey, who had been one of my teachers when I was a cadet, looked at me as though I had gone mad.

'My dear Bingle,' he said, using my army nickname, 'How on earth do you expect to absorb a bunch of civilians of that calibre into a military establishment? And how do you expect to pay them?'

I was ready for this and had previously drafted a paper suggesting how my scheme might be carried out. I thought we could form a civilian cadre of instructors especially for the academy. I proposed they be given Military rank for pay and allowances but in a special cadre for service only in the Academy. They would not wear uniform, of course, but civilian clothes with academic gowns on top, which might make it easier for them to accept employment in a military environment; it would also emphasize their status and learning and could only have a good effect on their students. As for pay, the military finance people would very likely prove resistant to the proposal that they should foot the bill for this civilian cadre; they would certainly spend weeks if not months in committee meetings. But we could not afford to wait so long. I wanted the Chief to go over their heads. He agreed, and put in a call to the Ministry of Defence in Karachi immediately. Again, Iskander Mirza came through, and I got the necessary permission.

I placed my advertisement that same day. We were swamped with applications from displaced and out-of-work academics. Most had several degrees; one gentlemen had doctorates in philosophy from Edinburgh, Bonn and Leiden universities. What a galaxy of talent – and all of them so eager for a job!

It was towards the end of 1947 that we got the final go-ahead to set up shop in Kakul. We now had the location, the beginnings of a curriculum and the staff. Our academic prospects looked excellent. But there was still plenty to be done before the first course at the Pakistan Military Academy could begin in January, 1948.

18

Setting Up Shop

The first cadets were due to arrive at the Academy in January, 1948, though the official opening would not be until late the following year. Before they arrived, I still faced a scramble to prepare their accommodation and sort out the various shortcomings at Kakul. Because of the shortage of funds I found myself continually having to beg, borrow and steal.

I had heard that the Pakistan Government had decided not to post any troops in tribal territory; this new policy meant the closure of two military posts, at Razmak and Wana, each of which housed a complete brigade group with officers' clubs and all the usual facilities. I wrote to the two brigade commanders and to the presidents of the officers' clubs, asking that they donate to the Academy all furniture, furnishings, crockery – in fact anything they no longer needed. Their response was magnificent: lorry-load after lorry-load arrived at Kakul; we now had adequate equipment to furnish all our messes. In addition they sent the crests of the two brigades which had been hanging in their respective clubs, as well as the regimental crests of other British units who had served there. All were accommodated at the Academy, and two of the cadet anterooms are known to this day as the Razmak and Wana Brigade Rooms.

Another problem at Kakul was that the former training school had had no need of a big parade ground, and had possessed only one soccer pitch, one hockey ground and a few volleyball courts. I wanted much more. To meet our needs and allow for future expansion, I wanted a parade ground large enough to accommodate two battalions, at least four soccer pitches and hockey grounds, courts for basketball as well as volleyball, and an Olympic-sized running track. The running track, I decided, could be built on the old golfcourse used by officers in the days of the Artillery School; but the terrain – though wide enough for all the facilities I wanted – was very uneven and would need to be excavated, in places to cut away the hillside on which the Academy stood. Where would I find all the heavy earth-moving monsters to do the work?

The idea came to me one day in the bar of the Pindi Officers' Club: I would steal a mechanical equipment platoon. It so happened that in this bar I met a young British engineer officer, looking rather downcast. I asked him what was wrong and discovered that his unit was about to be disbanded. He was due to return to England and would have to leave behind his Punjabi 'Mussulmans' as he called them.

'They're a great lot,' he said, reminiscing about their recent spell in Burma. 'I shall miss them.'

I struck while the iron was hot. 'How would you like to give your men a real send off – a *burra khana* (big feast)?'

If he could move his whole outfit up to Kakul, I told him, and work like hell for a week, I would arrange a *burra khana* they'd remember for the rest of their lives. As Commandant of the Academy I assured him I would fix it with AHQ. I suppose my red tabs impressed him; anyway, he agreed to my scheme with alacrity.

Before noon the following day, the young engineer officer and his whole unit had turned up at Kakul – with all their big bulldozers, graders and other heavy plant. And they did a marvellous job; within a few days the Academy had acquired all the flat terrain it needed. I was delighted – and so were his men, for I kept my promise and laid on a memorable *burra khana*.

Unfortunately the whole affair came out when I had to ask the AHQ accounts people for money to tarmac the new parade ground. Because I had not had the authority to order the engineering unit's movement, AHQ was not best pleased with me. They totted up the cost of moving the men and all their machinery, both to Kakul and back to Rawalpindi, the oil and petrol consumed, even the wear and tear on the equipment. Then they sent me a bill for 104,000 rupees and said they would take it out of my pay!

I chanced to be meeting the Prime Minister, Mr Liaquat Ali Khan, just after the bill arrived, and I made a clean breast of the whole business. He laughed, teasing me about all the rumours he'd heard of my 'organized looting' session in schools and colleges and about my reputation for treading on certain toes if I couldn't get what I wanted.

'Give me the bill, you *dakoo* (bandit),' he smiled. 'That is one of the better stories of the founding of our country. You won't hear any more about it. By the way, where did you get the funds to pay for the *burra khana*? Or did you come by those illicitly too?'

No, I told him, that had been perfectly aboved board. A few weeks after arriving in Pakistan I had asked for leave to visit India on urgent business. As I well knew, Pakistan was supposed to get one-third of all India's assets. I also knew we should never get our share of the Indian Military Academy; how could one divide it anyway? But the private funds were another matter. I flew to Delhi, wangled a staff car out of the GHQ pool and drove to Dehra Dun where the IMA was located. I knew the outgoing British Commandant was still there and I persuaded him to let me have our share of the private funds. It was only about four thousand rupees, but enough to start us off. There was a slight hold-up about the release of the money, and I had to appeal to Major-General Kalwant Singh, the new Indian CGS; he had been one of the Directing Staff when I was a student at the Staff College in Quetta. Finally I got the money and put it into Grindlay's Bank in New Delhi, who transferred it to an account I opened for the academy in their branch in Peshawar.

The PM just said: 'You ought to be in business.'

By late 1947 I was dividing my time between AHQ in Rawalpindi and the Academy in Kakul. One or two of the instructors had already moved in, and a dozen or so soldiers who were doing guard duty over the premises and stores. We were slightly nervous that the Academy might be raided, for trouble had broken out in Kashmir and we were only a few miles from the border.

It had all begun in October when the tribesmen of the old North West Frontier Province had banded together and, seizing advantage of the post-Partition confusion, invaded Kashmir. Hari Singh, the Maharaja of Kashmir, had been dithering over his right to opt for either India or Pakistan or to remain independent, a legal option all ruling princes had under the Partition Laws. The majority population of his state was Muslim; on the other hand, he himself and the Kashmiri intelligentsia were all Hindus. While he dithered, the massed tribes invaded. Afridi, Mahsud and Wahzir, all had been fighting the British for generations; they were well armed and they lived for loot and destruction. This was all a long way from Karachi and the Government of Pakistan; apparently they had heard nothing of the trouble brewing up on the borders, hence their decision to withdraw troops from the tribal areas. But this decision had repercussions that are still being felt today.

The massed tribesmen surged into Kashmir and could have reached the capital, Srinagar, with virtually no opposition; but they paused to sack the town of Baramulla and rape and kill the nuns in a convent there. Meanwhile the Indian Government had been pressurizing Hari Singh; he opted to take his state into India, and within hours the Indian Army was in his country, blocking the roads to the capital. Gradually they drove the tribesman back out of Kashmir.

The Government of Pakistan was outraged. Kashmir, the Pakistanis felt, belonged to them; after all, over 90% of the people were Muslim. They saw the Indian Army presence in Kashmir as a personal insult. There was an outcry for a *jehad* (holy war) and units of the Pakistan Army raced north to confront the Indians. The situation was referred for arbitration to the United Nations; while there was no official state of war between India and Pakistan, there were frequent outbreaks of fighting.

The tribesmen, meanwhile, drifted slowly back to their homelands bordering Afghanistan, some of them passing through Abbottabad. Totally undisciplined – their *maliks* (leaders) had little or no control of them – they arrived in bands of a hundred or so, firing their rifles in the streets and at one point commandeering the bazaar, helping themselves to whatever they fancied. The local police, under-strength and with few experienced senior officers, were incapable of tackling these tough bandits. For a while it looked as if they might raid Kakul as well, a mere five miles away. But gradually most moved on, heading for their homelands. The local people, however, the Shinwaris, had been unsettled by all these events. Some of them staged a minor raid on Kakul. I happened to be away at the time, and it was not till the next day that I found out what happened.

Among the first staff officers to arrive at the Academy had been Colonel Attiquar Rahman, my Chief Instructor. He was a very able man and I had been lucky to get him. His father was a very distinguished physician who, with his wife and family, had been living in southern India where he had spent many years in the service of the Nizam of Hyderabad. Dr Rahman and his wife had only just arrived in Pakistan and, like many other Muslim refugees, had been forced to abandon all their worldly goods – except for Mrs Rahman's jewellery. While they stayed with their son at Kakul, Mrs Rahman kept her jewels under the bed. Someone, probably a servant, must have tipped off the Shinwaris. They raided the place and found the jewels. But they had been heard in Mrs Rahman's bedroom. Several officers rushed in and three of the interlopers were caught, but the others made off with the bulk of the loot.

Naturally everyone at Kakul was mad as hell. I am not making excuses but the situation got completely out of hand. It must be remembered that these were very troubled times and mayhem was the order of the day. The officers undoubtedly misbehaved: allegedly, they tortured the three prisoners using rubber hoses and lighted cigarettes, and locked them in the military guardroom. Never, never do you lock civilians in a military guardroom. The following day I arrived at Kakul and went to my office, but no one mentioned the incident to me; I still had no inkling of the affair. That same day the officers decided to take their prisoners up the hill to Colonel Rahman's bungalow for further interrogation at the scene of the crime. The inevitable happened: the three Shinwaris made a break for freedom. They ran into the path of a convoy of trucks coming down the hill at a fair speed, and one man was run over; another jumped into a twenty-foot chasm and broke a leg, while the third was recaptured uninjured.

The convoy of trucks stopped and the junior NCO in command of the convoy sent for his commanding officer in Abbottabad. No one, alas, thought to send for me. The story reached Abbottabad within minutes and spread all over the bazaar. Soon a couple of hundred tribals were advancing on Kakul. The Superintendent of Police had also heard the story and had the guts to collect a couple of sepoys and follow the procession to Kakul.

All unaware of this time bomb, I was in my office at work. Suddenly I heard the noise of firing on the hill outside. I sent for my battalion adjutant. I still had no suspicion of the real cause of the trouble; I believe I thought some sepoy had gone berserk and was running around firing his rifle at all and sundry.

A minute later the battalion adjutant joined me – Captain 'Killer' Mehdi, a great chap and steady as a rock.

'What the hell goes on, Killer?'

'Don't really know, sir. Sounds like .303 fire to me.'

'Dammit, man, get cracking! Get my jeep.'

We jumped into the jeep and roared off down the hill. Halfway down, bang in the middle of the road, was this mass of humanity. I couldn't believe my eyes. Tribals seemed to be everywhere. As we drove up I saw the Superintendent of Police; he was leaning helplessly against the front of a truck, looking as white as a sheet, and his two sepoys stood alongside him. All had been disarmed. Their rifles had been grabbed as soon as they stepped out of the policeman's car.

The crowd was in an ugly mood. They surged towards us as Mehdi stopped the jeep, firing their guns in the air and yelling at us. Neither Mehdi nor I were armed but we plunged through their midst to speak to the policeman and find out what was going on. Eventually I discovered that a Shinwari had been run over by the army truck, though it was not till later that I understood why. I grabbed the nearest man and asked where the corpse was.

'Picche (on the back),' he said tersely, indicating the rear of the truck.

With considerable misgiving I walked round the truck. The corpse was dripping from the tailboard, a very unlovely sight: half the head was missing and there was blood everywhere. Now I could see why the assembled multitude was screaming for retribution. I climbed on the tailboard and stood for a moment looking down at them: thugs, covered in bandoliers, knives, pistols and rifles. Other than through the sights of a .303 rifle, I was probably the first British officer they had ever seen face to face. Their idea of fun was to kill one of my race, emasculate him and stuff his genitals in his mouth. I wasn't quite ready for that kind of meal.

Shakespeare put a great speech into Mark Antony's mouth, but I think I matched him that day. While I knew most of my audience spoke Pashto, I had to speak in Urdu as I didn't know any Pashto, and anyway Urdu was the language of Pakistan. I spoke of Muslim heroes: the Quaid-i-Azam, Khalid, Tariq, the lot. I promised a full enquiry conducted by the Governor-General himself. I promised a slap-up funeral for the victim and a *burra-khana* afterwards for the mourners. At last the message got through to them; they decided I was something new and strange – a British officer who was on their side. There were murmurs of '*Shahbash*' (Bravo, good).

I looked round for Mehdi, who was not far away and still supporting me nobly. I jumped down from the tailboard, joined him and returned to the jeep. Gradually the crowd was beginning to disperse. With a sigh of relief, we picked up the Superintendent of Police and retreated to the Academy. I phoned the Deputy Commissioner in Abbottabad and reported what had happened. He rallied round immediately; he sent his men out into the bazaar and collected vast quantities of food, then arranged for a contractor to have the food cooked in a field adjacent to the cemetery.

At sundown that day we all assembled at the burial ground and the corpse was interred. There were speeches galore, including another briefer one from myself – again promising a fully-fledged enquiry. This would have been normal procedure in a case of this nature, but the investigation was taken out of the hands of the military, on orders from Karachi, and an interminable civil enquiry was launched under the auspices of the North West Frontier Government. It was still not concluded when I left Pakistan in 1951. Needless to say, a lot of politics were involved and I think the Army would have done a cleaner and quicker job. Later I heard that all the officers alleged to be involved were exonerated. So ended a very messy day. I was glad to come out of it with a whole skin.

As the first Commandant of the new Academy I felt it was my duty not only to get the show rolling, so to speak, and start a steady flow of young officers into the Pakistan Army, but also to ensure that the institution would instil a certain esprit de corps in the cadets. To this end I had to find some way of inspiring them – creating a tradition that would provide them with a sense of heritage, something of which they could be proud.

Pakistan, of course, had no history or tradition. The state was only a few months old. The concept of a land called Pakistan ('Land of the Pure') is said to have originated in the 1920s – the dream of Iqbal the poet. The dream was now reality, and reality meant a fledgling country without a common heritage. Except for one thing: the vast majority of Pakistanis were of the Muslim faith. The Academy's inspiration, I therefore decided, must come from the great Muslim culture and traditions, fourteen hundred years old.

The idea came to us to name the four companies of the Cadet Battalion after those great Muslim heroes of the past: Khalid, Tariq, Kasim and Salahuddin (or Saladin, as we have anglicized the name). The idea soon caught on. As I had hoped, the cadets seized upon and cherished the names of their respective companies and when there was inter-company rivalry on the sports field the hillsides of Kakul rang with their calls of 'Khalid!' or 'Taliq!' and so on. Each company was immediately clothed with a personality of its own and the beginnings of a great esprit were born. Later, to carry the idea further, I decided to give the battalion itself a title and personality of its own. Mr Jinnah, leader of the Muslim League in British India and founder of Pakistan, had become Quaid-i-Azam (Father of the Nation), a title of great respect; I now asked the C-in-C to propose to Mr Jinnah that the Cadet Battalion be named 'the Quaid-i-Azam's Own' and designated the senior battalion in the Pakistan Army. And this was approved.

The next step was to get colours designed and presented. Regimental colours have always been the outward and visible sign of the spirit and honour of a regiment; the greatest dishonour a unit could suffer was the loss of its colours in battle. Today they are no longer carried on active service, but still the regimental spirit is enshrined in them. When new colours are presented there is a special ceremony, blessing them before they are handed over by some distinguished person. Traditionally all British and Imperial Indian Army battalions carried two colours: the King's Colour, embroidered and usually with the battalion's number in the centre, and the Battalion Colour; the latter might be in the colour of the unit's facings, and on the flag was embroidered the battle honours granted the battalion in past campaigns. It was decided the PMA's Cadet Battalion would also have two colours.

A committee was set up at AHQ to discuss the question of the colours; I was a member and the chairman was the Pakistani Adjutant-General. We came up with two very attractive designs, one of which incorporated the Union Jack, for at this time, of course, Pakistan was a British Dominion and theoretically at least King George VI was King of Pakistan. None of the Pakistanis on the committee thought to question the appropriateness of this design – not even the chairman. I certainly did not. The two designs were sent for manufacture to the Royal School of Needlework in London. I don't know who gave the designs the final approval, but as I discovered much later it was not the Minister of Defence in Karachi.

It was intended that the colours be presented by the Quaid-i-Azam in person at the Academy's official opening ceremony in late 1949. Unfortunately Mr Jinnah died in September, 1948. In any case, the flags did not reach us until after the opening ceremony – and when they did at last arrive from England they were to cause me profound chagrin. But that was two years away.

On 26 January, 1948, I made my first address to the staff and assembled 'gentlemen cadets' – I had borrowed the term from Sandhurst – of the Pakistan Military Academy, the cradle of the future Pakistan Army. It was a proud moment for all of us.

The organizational chores continued, however, and I had to keep the training going at top speed; but there were moments when my mind turned to various intriguing matters – such as a badge for the Cadet Battalion, now named 'The 1st Pakistan Battalion, the Quaid-i-Azam's Own'. I fooled around with pieces of squared paper and finally came up with a design that pleased me. To my delight, this was approved at AHQ, with one exception: we still needed a motto to go with the badge. Another committee was set up, this one consisting of soldiers, scholars and *moulvis* (Muslim religious teachers) and after a week or two they selected a suitable passage from the *Koran Sharif*, the Muslim holy book: '*Nasroon minihalhi wah fatroon qarib*', roughly interpreted as 'When God is with you then victory is near'. As the C-in-C's military secretary, Jim Wilson of the Rifle Brigade, said rather facetiously, 'I always thought it was better to have God "under command" rather than "in support" ' – a reference to familiar battle terms.

Another requirement leading to flights of artistic fancy was for an Academy magazine. This, of course, was something I could delegate to others, but it was I who coined its name. One evening I was standing in my garden, gazing at the high mountains that formed such a beautiful backdrop to the Academy, and as I watched a silvery new moon appeared over the snowy peaks. There was the name for our magazine, I thought: 'The Rising Crescent'. I hoped it was symbolic of the new academy's future.

Between my more onerous duties there were many other aspects of Academy life in which I dabbled. At one stage I had acquired some heavy wooden-wheeled bullock carts, and now I had them stripped and lightened, then fitted with old car axles and pneumatic-tyred wheels; they carried a far heavier payload than the wooden-wheeled variety and were much easier for the animals to pull on the steep Kakul hills. Another time I bought some sheep and organized them on a profit-making basis. The grazing was good and the shepherds' pay was minimal. As the sheep were slaughtered they were sold to the mess contractor; thus the cadets got good meat and we built up the Academy's private funds.

Reluctantly I had been forced to concede that there was no case to be made for riding on the curriculum. But I was determined we shouldn't do without horses altogether; I have always believed that horsemanship is a great asset to an officer, giving him poise and confidence and an eye for country. Besides, the Burma campaign in the Second World War had proved that, in certain terrain at least, the day of the horse was far from over. I had heard that many ponies had been categorized as surplus to needs after the war, so I made a few discreet enquiries to find out what had happened to them. I discovered that the nearby remount depots of Mona and Sargodha were holding quite a large number. I forget what phoney excuse I used to get them, but I soon had forty ponies, together with orderlies, grooms and equipment, on the Academy establishment. I selected them personally; all were of a suitable temperament, make and shape for polo. I founded a riding school in Kakul, which cadets were able to join upon payment of a small fee; soon our embryo horsemen were riding all over the local countryside.

We also started a little stick and ball practice on the polo grounds of Abbottabad, and in no time I found I could put together quite a respectable polo side: at first two cadets, one of the remount NCOs and myself, later three cadets and myself. And in those days, when few regiments had had the opportunity to organize themselves for polo, we made a strong combination. In fact, we often walked away the winners at tournaments in Abbottabad, even in Rawalpindi and Peshawar.

Step by step, one small achievement after another, the PMA was beginning to take on a life and character of its own. I found it very satisfying. But even so, there were constant and innumerable complications.

19

Complications at Kakul

While the Hazara District, in which Kakul was located, was inhabited by a tribal people whose religion was Islam, Abbottabad and the larger villages had been home to a large colony of Sikhs and Hindus. Many were shopkeepers or moneylenders; many others performed menial tasks such as those of washermen and sweepers (disposers of excreta and other noisome residue) that no one else would touch. When first I decided on Kakul as the site of the PMA I believed that all Hindus and Sikhs had either been killed or had left for India. I was wrong. Soon after I moved into the Commandant's House, Adalat Khan, my Muslim bearer for many years, came into my room one day and informed me that a *dhobi* (washerman) was requesting an interview. We needed a *dhobi* to look after the household laundry, and I had been wondering where one might be found, so I told Adalat to bring him in. When Adalat returned he was ushering before him a wizened little man wearing a *dhoti* (loincloth), a garment worn exclusively by Hindus.

I was amazed: a Hindu in Kakul! I thought he had come to ask for my protection. Not so. Speaking with great dignity, he explained that he had come to pay his respects to me as the new Commanding Officer, just as he had always done in the past whenever a new *pultan* (battalion) came to Kakul. His father had been the *dhobi* here, and his father before him; his wife was dead and his children had fled to India. But he was not afraid: 'If they kill me, it will be because my time has come.' In the meantime he wanted to stay as my *dhobi*.

'If I may serve you,' he finished, 'I will always pray for Your Honour's

131

long life and prosperity.' And he placed his hands together and bowed his head over them in the traditional attitude of obeisance.

I was much moved by his faith and dignity. He was of indeterminate age but looked wiry enough, capable of doing a full day's work. I agreed to give him the job as my personal *dhobi*. Adalat took him under his wing and gave him a quarter close to the house. He was still there, washing sheets and pillowcases on the rocks, when I left three years later. My Muslim servants were kind to him and bought his grain and vegetables in the bazaar so that he never had to leave the compound and be exposed to the ruffians of Abbottabad who surely would have killed him.

Later I heard of many other good deeds performed by honest people during this troubled time, but alas, they were few and far between; the acts of bestiality outnumbered them by far. I was proud of Adalat Khan and my other Muslim servants for their acts of charity and kindness.

But as a foreigner and non-Muslim, I had to think very carefully before deciding on certain matters which the Commandant of a military academy in his own country and among his own people would never have to face. I had served with Muslim soldiers for years in the Indian Imperial Army and therefore had some acquaintance with their religious beliefs and customs. I had also read much of the *Koran Sharif*, in an English translation, and on accepting the appointment as Commandant of the PMA had taken the Precaution of brushing up my knowledge of the tenets of Islam. But I still found it wise to tread warily.

For example, during my first few months in command we faced the Muslim holy month of Ramzan. Throughout Ramzan Muslims are expected to fast from sunrise to sunset, and I wondered if this might cause problems with our work schedule. I called a conference of my senior instructors to discuss the matter, reminding them that our first priority was to train officers for the Pakistan Army and commission them on time.

At first there was silence in the room. My regular officers were waiting for the Director of Studies to speak: Lieutenant-Colonel Dr M. M. Ahmed, one of the special 'officer civilians' I had recruited. Dr Ahmed was very orthodox and he obviously felt out of his depth in this military environment, so far removed from the peaceful world of students and academics. He looked at me with a pained expression; I had to take pity on him. Far better that I should state my case, then allow modifications to emerge in discussion afterwards. So, with some temerity, I launched into the deep water.

First of all I made it plain that there would be no deviation of either day or night work as scheduled for the month; equally that I expected the fast to be kept within the meaning of the Good Book – but, as I understood it, the Holy Prophet himself permitted certain exceptions. Those who were sick or were on a journey or had a special task to perform might break the fast in moderation. I looked around the room; everyone was nodding agreement.

'All right,' I went on, 'we have four cadet company messes and the officers' mess. During Ramzan, all except one mess shall remain closed. In that one mess, food will be available throughout the day for those who feel they cannot complete their workload without it. Is that agreeable?'

The look of relief on their faces was answer enough. It was agreed.

My arrangements could not have worked in a more satisfactory manner. On the first two days of the fast the open mess had no customers during the daylight hours; but on the following days there began a trickle, and after ten days quite a number found they could not go the pace and fast as well.

Fasting was not the only requirement during Ramzan, for Muslims also had to abstain from tobacco. It was understood that any cadet or officer found having a surreptitious drag at a cigarette during fasting hours would be on a charge. I spoke to all my non-Muslim staff and made it plain that during Ramzan there would be no smoking in public, not even in the comparative privacy of administrative offices. In those days I was a heavy smoker, but I applied the rule to myself as well; I'm sure it gave my lungs a breather.

My readers must remember that the state of Pakistan, carved out of British India, was still only a few months old. The vast majority of its people were of the Muslim faith, although there were a few Hindus left and a number of Christians. In the early days there were some who wanted the land to be governed according to the tenets of the Shariat law; for example, death for adulterers, the loss of a hand for theft, and a total ban on the sale and use of alcohol. The majority of the intelligentsia were not for Shariat law, however, but rather for continuance of the British system of law which had been in force in the subcontinent for about two hundred years. At the same time, most people did accept a more stringent code of social and moral behaviour now, and a closer observance of the basic requirements of Islam.

It is the tradition in Muslim countries for all married ladies and ladies of marriageable age to observe *purdah*, the wearing of the veil. In some families the ladies lived in a separate part of the house and never appeared without the veil in front of any male who was not a part of the family. Most of my married Muslim staff had served in regiments with British commanding officers and with brother officers who were British; wanting to share in the social activities of the regiment, they therefore encouraged their womenfolk to forsake the veil and join in the normal life of the station. But I did have a number of instructors who were rather straightlaced, both socially and religiously, and who were not accustomed to letting their wives appear unveiled in public.

It was here that the two sophisticated sisters from Bhopal came to my aid. One married to Colonel Latif Khan, my deputy, the other to Major Abid Bilgrami, a company commander, they did much to help the wives of other officers and staff, particularly those who came from very orthodox Muslim backgrounds. I explained to these two ladies that I wanted to encourage my cadets and their future families to play the fullest possible role in their country's affairs, so the staff should set them an appropriate example. I was anxious to avoid offending anyone's religious susceptibilities and would not countenance any attempt to force the orthodox ladies to relinquish the veil; on the other hand they needed to be shown that a new day had dawned and that they could not help in the establishment of their country by remaining hidden in the women's quarters. This the Bhopal sisters understood; as well as organizing the social life of the Academy, they began gently to emancipate their sisters.

I formed a Ladies' Welfare Committee and requested the organizers to see that all the *purdah* ladies were included in its activities. For example, early in 1948 the Welfare Committee organized a *meena bazaar* (jumble sale) in the grounds of the officers' mess. Of course, all the ladies made goods and sweetmeats for sale, including those in *purdah*, for this sale was in aid of the Kashmir Refugees' Relief Fund; donations to and support of this fund were almost a matter of national honour to the Pakistanis, who considered that the plight of the refugees was caused solely by the Indian invasion of Kashmir. So I informed all of my officers whose ladies were in *purdah* that I expected them to do their part of the *meena bazaar* and to make an appearance; special arrangements would be made to sequester them in a screened-off corner of the garden and after that it was up to them.

The party started well, with people coming from all over the valley to attend. There were games, prizes and auctions. The *purdah* ladies could get only fleeting glimpses of the fun by peering through the gaps in the screens behind which they had hid themselves. After a while I noticed that one of the screens had been moved, then that one or two of the ladies were actually mingling with the throng – albeit heavily draped in their *burkhas* (a sort of tent-like affair with slits for the eyes). Later, I saw that one at least had joined a group of unveiled ladies and lifted her own veil. So we were making progress.

It was the same in our cinemas. First the *purdah* ladies demanded a special screened off area, which I duly arranged, though not in the best viewing area. Then I noticed that some were moving out of this area into seats of their own choice, though still in *burkha*. After some weeks one or two were sitting in the stalls with their veils actually lifted, only covering their faces when the lights went up in the interval. Gradually some of the younger ones forsook the veil altogether, and, as I had hoped, began to play a much more active part in the academy's social life. It was, I knew, largely thanks to the encouragement of the two Bhopal sisters, whose activities contributed so much to the cohesion and happiness of the staff and cadets of the Academy.

Our efforts, however, were not universally appreciated as I was to discover.

There was a local group of *maulvis* (religious teachers) in Abbottabad who were always preaching that hell and damnation would overcome the Academy and myself. They did not approve of the fact that most of our ladies did not wear the veil or that many of my Muslim staff were accustomed to take a drink once in a while. They were aided and abetted by a local character, a small-time thug and conman who lived in the village of Jadote, about ten miles from the Academy on the road to Murree. It was a typical village of the smaller sort – about three or four mud-built huts called *bastis* clinging to the hillside – but the impudent fellow had granted himself an illusory title: Khan Faquira Khan, Khan of Jadote.

Our friend was a rather typical Pathan of the baser sort. Tall, with a shaven head under his *kullah* and *pagri*, he was a heavyweight in most senses of the term. It was said that he had at least twelve murders on his hands. With the advent of Partition, however, he had thought he would become a leading figure in the district. He hoped, by siding with the militant *maulvis*, to achieve more local influence, and published a disreputable bazaar newspaper, the *Inkishaf*, in which he called for total governance of Pakistan by Islamic Shariat law.

The man became a constant thorn in my flesh, regularly calling at my private residence with some request or grievance. He would push his turban back over his hennaed side hairs and say in English: 'Now, my dear *Jenail Saab* (General Sahib) . . .' and then lapse into Urdu to express his demands. No amount of coolness on my part could deter him. Eventually I was constrained to lodge a complaint with the Deputy Commissioner of his district and request that he be banned from the Academy grounds. The following day his rag came out with a banner headline: 'BRIGADIER BARS LOCAL KHAN FROM OUR NATIONAL ACADEMY!' He stirred up quite a mare's nest of protest in the bazaars of Abbottabad, in the course of which the local riff-raff burned down the Officers' Club in the Abbottabad cantonment. More headlines: 'ENGLISH CLUB BURNS TO THE GROUND! PAKISTANI OFFICERS AND THEIR WOMEN SEEN RUNNING NAKED FROM THE FLAMES!' For good measure he reported that, with his own eyes, he had seen me swimming alone with Pakistani ladies in the officers' mess pool at the Academy.

It was all getting too much, so I sent for him to my house and read him a lecture on nationalism, since he claimed to be a nationalist, and told him how he was damaging our urgent business at the Academy. He was like a little boy who had been caught in a practical joke. I told him that, if he continued to play the fool, I would see to it that he would never attend a function at the Academy – for this was all he was after, the kudos of meeting our distinguished visitors.

My words must have done the trick. He changed tack completely and his newspaper started printing laudatory articles about the PMA. He ceased to pester me, so when the Governor-General came to visit I rewarded him with a seat at the reception. To judge by his reaction one would have thought I had made him a Nawab. Soon afterwards he died in rather mysterious circumstances – sent to his just reward by a well-wisher, no doubt.

Not all of the local gentry were as tiresome as Khan Faquira Khan. Many were kind and hospitable. During one of the between-term breaks, my wife and I accepted an invitation to visit Amb, a fortified town about eighty miles north-west of Attock Fort, located in a gorge above the River Indus. The town was built around the palace of the Nawab of Amb, a minor prince who in those days ruled over a few hundred square miles of lofty and almost impenetrable mountains. Until 1947 most of the business people and shopkeepers of the town of Amb were either Sikh or Hindu, many of whom had fled to India at Partition; the revenues of the state had suffered as a result. The Nawab was a most amiable and tolerant man – but only as far as his friends and subjects were concerned; for years he had been at odds with his neighbouring states of Dir and Swat. There was a saying in this frontier state that all disputes were caused by *Zan, Zer, Zamin* (Women, Jewels or Land); in the Nawab of Amb's case it was land.

The roads were almost nonexistent, more like cart tracks and barely suitable for cars. So it was after a slow, hot and dusty trip that my wife, Heather, and I arrived in Amb. We were met by a guard of honour and a nondescript band playing the most outlandish tunes. Then we were welcomed at a reception where as usual there were no other woman present; my wife became an object of fascination among the other guests, many of whom had never seen a white woman before. After the customary exchange of speeches we were shown to our rooms in the palace – very primitive but clean, with tiny windows overlooking the valley. Under each bed was the inevitable 'peespat' and on the bedside table stood a bottle of Johnnie Walker Black Label. Perhaps our host assumed that no Englishman could survive the business of the day without a shot of scotch. In some cases he may well have been right.

That evening we were bidden to an early supper, as we were told that the fighting had intensified between the Nawab and his current enemy, the

136

Nawab of Dir, and that some of the notables might have to leave for the front before nightfall. Dinner was sumptuous: mountains of *pulao*, goat's meat curry and kebabs followed by sherbet and all sorts of sticky sweets. After dinner the so-called court jester came in to entertain us; he was a gnome-like little man of uncertain age but with a great twinkle in his eyes and I guessed some of his Pathan songs were not for the ears of a lady – but as she could not understand them it did not matter. He had just regaled us with his one and only English language song, 'I will buy you a packet of pins', when the Prime Minister of Amb burst into the room in a state of great agitation. The performance stopped and he prostrated himself before the ruler. When given permission to speak, he produced a schoolboy's copy-book from which he read the latest dispatch from the front. The news was not good: it seemed the enemy had penetrated about five miles into Amb territory.

Our host seemed not at all upset. Calmly he took us all out to a courtyard to watch him muster his forces. In the late evening sunlight I watched in growing fascination as two field guns were trundled forward for inspection. One was stamped with the maker's mark – Krupp – but the other one, though it lacked the stamp, looked identical. I asked the Nawab about the two guns. Apparently the one with the stamp had been captured from the Turks in the First World War and afterwards had been presented to the Nawab, in recognition of his services, by the Government of India. The Indians had intended the gun to be used purely for decorative purposes, but the wily Nawab had a better idea. He found a blacksmith who not only made this museum piece operable, but also copied it exactly and constructed a second gun. As the original had been designed to fire a 'separate charge' rather than a single shell, they were able to use their own fabricated ammunition: black powder and bags of old nails or nuts and bolts. The calibre was quite small, about the equivalent of a British thirteen-pounder of that era, but it was a formidable weapon as well as a work of art.

Still marvelling at the untutored craftsmanship of the copy, I turned to my host and asked how his men would get the guns into action; after all, the terrain was not exactly suitable. He told me he had plenty of strong young men who could manhandle them up the steepest mountains; in any case, this time they didn't have far to go.

'We have enticed the enemy into an enclosed valley,' he explained. 'There is a small hill overlooking the valley and when my men get there with the guns, then – poof! We shall blow them all to Gehenna (hell)!'

Another visit I made was to the Nawab of Amb's other traditional enemy, the Wali of Swat. I had known the Wali, Major-General Miangul Jahanzeb, for some years and his son was in the first batch of cadets at Kakul. Waliahd Miangul Aurungzeb, the heir apparent, was an excellent cadet, an under-officer and runner up for the Sword of Honour. After he graduated his father invited us to visit the state of Swat.

Swat lies north of the Malakand Pass with Russian Turkestan as its northern neighbour. It was at Malakand, in the latter part of the last century, that Winston Churchill got his first job as a war correspondent with the Malakand Field Force. And, according to tradition, it was near the Malakand Pass that the incident occurred that led Rudyard Kipling to write his poem about the water-carrier, Gunga Din. Since those days the Swatis had been loyal subjects of the British Crown, and today of Pakistan. The Swat valley is beautiful and water and game are abundant; the climate is equable all year round, though the surrounding hills are covered with snow in winter.

This visit was a much more sophisticated affair. Arriving in the capital of Saidu Sharif we found ourselves staying in the princely guesthouse, which looked as though it had been furnished by Liberty's of London. That afternoon our host took us out duck-shooting, for many waterfowl spent the summer months in the valley. We crouched inside carefully constructed, natural-looking hides, waiting for the birds to fly – it is considered unsportsmanlike to shoot a duck sitting on the water, hence the expression 'a sitting duck' – and towards the evening the ducks and geese duly began to return from feeding in the fields. There were no gundogs to retrieve the birds; each hide had a couple of local men who splashed happily through the water and retrieved as efficiently as any spaniel.

Among other distractions our host laid on, apart from picnics in the lovely countryside up on the Russian-Kashmiri borders, were golf (on a half-completed golfcourse) and a visit to the emerald mines. I still have an emerald tie-pin with the very stone I saw being dug out of the ground in the valley of Swat.

That first year at the Academy had almost finished by the time we had the official opening, on 25 November, 1949. It all went very well – but of course the main event, the whole purpose of our existence, was the first passing out parade on 4 February, 1950. This important ceremony was to be attended by vast numbers of guests, including the most important in the land: Mr Liaquat Ali Khan, who was both Prime Minister and Minister of Defence. He it was who would finally present the colours to the Cadet Battalion.

I made a special trip to Rawalpindi to collect the flags, newly arrived from the Royal School of Needlework in London. They were magnificent. The Battalion Colour was of Pakistan green, mounted on a staff with a brass-tipped spike, while the King's Colour featuring the Union Jack was on a staff tipped with a crown. Both were trimmed with a fringe of gold and were encased for travel in leather sheaths. I returned to Kakul in high spirits.

Our preparations for the parade were complete at last, even the tricky business of the seating plan which had to accord with precedence and protocol. The PM and his wife, the Begum Liaquat, were to stay in my private residence and the day before the ceremony I was beset by a swarm of secret service agents who checked on all my servants, looked up every chimney and peered into every bush in the garden. All was well, however, and in addition to their presence a ceremonial guard was posted at the house.

On the evening before the big event I had planned a dinner party for the PM and his wife, and about a dozen other guests including the senior members of my staff. When the PM arrived I took him to the drawing-room, while the Begum retired to her quarters, and wondered whether he would like a drink. I knew he was a pretty liberal man but orthodox Muslim groups were increasingly vocal in their opposition to alcohol. But, charming and tactful as ever, he simply asked what the custom was in my officers' mess. With the exception of one of my senior officers, all were accustomed to drink liquor; but I simply said that we served all kinds of drinks in the officers' mess and I left it up to individuals to decide.

'Good,' he said. 'May I have a whisky and soda?'

Before the others arrived for dinner we talked about the next day's parade, and the PM remarked on the excellent progress we had made at the Academy. By the time dinner was served I was feeling this was a pretty good day. My cook had produced an excellent meal; everyone was relaxed and at ease. The PM was asking what was expected of him during the ceremony tomorrow, and I sketched out the timing and what would happen when he reached the parade ground.

'And when the time comes to present the colours,' I went on, 'I will escort you forward, together with the Cadet Battalion Commander, the Commander-in-Chief and the Regimental Sergeant-Major. There are two colours, the King's Colour and—'

The PM choked and his face went purple. 'Brigadier Ingall, are you seriously telling me that you expect me to present a KING's Colour? I would remind you that Pakistan is a sovereign state – we owe no allegiance to the King!'

Needless to say, after that the soufflé was as flat as last week's rice pudding. As soon as the dinner was over I told the Battalion Commander to get the colours up to my house in double-quick time. In very short order Mr Duffield and the Battalion Adjutant appeared and, with much stamping and saluting, Mr Duffield revealed the standards to the PM. I did my best to explain the reason the AHQ committee had decided on a King's Colour, but had to admit that I didn't know who had given the design the final approval. The PM was not to be mollified.

'I'm not going to present that flag tomorrow,' he said, 'not to anyone anywhere in Pakistan.'

I was shattered. It was after 9.30 in the evening and the ceremony was due to commence at 9 am the following morning. Mr Duffield was marvellous: 'Not to worry, sir, I'll have it all squared away by parade time.' He and the Adjutant and the colours disappeared into the darkness. I returned to my drawing-room to what I thought would be a very awkward atmosphere. Not a bit of it. In my absence, Begum Liaquat had ordered my Chief Instructor to send for our two portable 16mm film projectors, as she wanted to see films about a refugee rehabilitation development. I suggested rather bleakly that we adjourn to the 16mm cinema.

'Oh no,' she replied brightly, 'it's much more comfortable here.'

My drawing-room was a shambles, everything topsy-turvy. I called for Adalat Khan to bring the drinks tray and attempted to make the best of a bad situation. The PM realized that I was upset and that the faux pas was not of my making, so we chatted lightly of other things while I kept my fingers crossed and tried to stop worrying about the morrow.

Mr Duffield rose to the occasion, as usual. When he left me he went to his office and sketched out an amended drill for the presentation of the Battalion Colour only. He had the colour party on parade at 6 am for rehearsal, and by the time the ceremony commenced all was in order. The passing out parade went off without a hitch. The rejected King's Colour reposed in the hallway of my house for some weeks, then I took it back to AHQ and handed it over to Major Wilson, the Chief's military secretary. I don't know what happened to it finally, but I have often regretted not keeping it as a memento.

I said the parade went off without a hitch. It was some days later that I received a charming letter from the PM, full of praise for the parade and my achievements at Kakul. However, there was a less welcome letter in the same mail. It was signed by a Mr Khan, a newly appointed Deputy Secretary in the Ministry of Defence on Karachi. Using the most vitriolic language he slanged me, my race, my inefficiency as Commandant, and bluntly accused me of being anti-Pakistani. Then he got down to the real reason for his complaint. He and his wife had been insulted at the ceremony. They had been seated in the third row back. Mr Khan thought he should have been seated in the front row.

Knowing how carefully we had arranged the seating plan, I was pretty sure of my ground, but, just to check, I sent for the staff officers who had been responsible for showing guests to their seats. Two of them remembered Mr Khan very well for he had created an almighty fuss when shown his allotted seat; he had demanded the place in the front row that had been reserved for the Governor of the North West Frontier Province. Rightly the

all General Gracey. We asked you here tonight so that you would indeed report all you have heard to the Chief.'

I took my leave with a heavy heart. Perhaps I should have dissuaded them – but it wouldn't have worked. They were full of revolutionary zeal. Apart from General Gracey's reaction, I suspected the Government in Karachi would take a dim view of a group of army officers trying to run the country. I was right. The following morning I went to Rawalpindi to see the Chief, and in my presence he telephoned the PM in Karachi to recount all that I had reported.

At first the Government's response was restrained. The officers were warned and told not to continue with their plot. But they went ahead just the same. One night the conspirators had arranged to meet at Attock Fort on the Kabul River – and the police were waiting for them. All were jailed; some of the most qualified and promising officers in the newly created country were lost to the professional army for ever.

Latif, too, was jailed: a great patriot, but misguided in his enthusiasm. He was ruined. When I last saw him in the 1960s he was the uncomfortable owner of a Shell Oil service station in Lahore.

My time at Kakul was coming to an end – surely the most constructive and creative period of my life. As Commandant of the PMA I had received many distinguished visitors: ambassadors, politicians, nawabs, members of the international press. I had played host to the Governor-General himself, His Excellency Alhaj Khwaja Nazimuddin, and to Miss Jinnah, sister of the Quaid-i-Azam who had so sadly died before ever seeing the Academy. The Prime Minister and the Begum Liaquat Ali Khan had stayed in my house – tragically his life was ended by a madman's bullet in October, 1951. Among my military visitors had been General Sir Frank Messervy, Commander-in-Chief of the Pakistan Army before General Gracey; Air Vice-Marshal Richard Atcherley, Commander-in-Chief of the Pakistan Air Force (and winner with his twin brother of the Schneider Trophy for Great Britain); Field-Marshal Sir William Slim, creator of victory in Burma in the Second World War and later Governor-General of Australia; and my former chief from the Indian Imperial Army, Field-Marshal Sir Claude Auchinleck. It was Field-Marshal Auchinleck who wrote to me after his visit:

I must congratulate you on what you have done and are doing for Pakistan. Unless I had seen it for myself I would not have believed it possible that the PMA should have become what it is in so short a time. It is almost a miracle!

But my agreement to serve Pakistan for three years would expire in August, 1950. Very naturally the Pakistanis wanted to run their own show, but there was some confusion and reluctance on the part of their Government to release new terms under which British officers might continue to serve. I also was somewhat confused as to my future. I had loved my time at Kakul; it was a fascinating job and I had always intended to serve out my active years as a soldier. But my army – the old Imperial Indian Army – no longer existed. I was not keen to go into the British Army as a second choice and any continued service in Pakistan could only be for a limited time. I was forty-one; if I were going to change my profession, delay could only be a disadvantage.

I received an offer from London to transfer into the Royal Tank Regiment, but it was clouded with if's and but's. Because I had commanded a regiment in war, I would never have the opportunity to command again; in other words, they didn't want to block one of their own for promotion. I would have to join them as a lieutenant-colonel, but due to my 'record and staff qualifications', they said, I might eventually become a brigadier on the staff. It was all too iffy.

At the same time I received a letter from the Military of Defence in Karachi asking if I would agree to another year's extension, until August, 1951. After all I had done, I must admit to feeling just a little hurt and vaguely insulted by this offer. Couldn't they see that a year out of my life now would be expensive to my future? I felt almost as if I were a lance-corporal being given a chance of an extra year before returning to civvy street. There were still too many 'time-servers' among the British officers hanging on in Pakistan; they should have been weeded out and those of us who were doing a constructive job should have been offered a worthwhile contract. At least our service in Pakistan could have counted towards our pension; I found now that it did not, though those who served on in India received such credit.

My long-range plan had always been to go into business; now seemed to be the time. I therefore declined all offers and regretfully wrote a formal letter to the War Office in London, requesting them to place it before His Majesty, praying that I be granted permission to resign my commission with effect from 1 January, 1951. In due course, formal permission was granted.

Meanwhile I had been making contacts. An old friend of mine – Leslie Sawhny, who had been my deputy at the Armoured Officers' Training School in Ahmednagar – had joined the long-established Far Eastern firm of Killick, Nixon & Co in Bombay. I wrote to him and he kindly arranged an interview with the board of directors in Bombay. Time was short, however; and although there was a regular flight between Karachi and Bombay, regular internal air services had not yet started in Pakistan. Fortunately another old friend turned up trumps: Air Marshal Atcherley, whom I had helped set up the Air Force Academy at Risalpur. He arranged for a service plane to fly me to Karachi, to catch the connection to Bombay, and back again afterwards.

My trip was a great success and I returned to Kakul with a contract in my pocket. All that was left was to pack up and say goodbye to so many good friends at the Academy. On New Year's Day, 1951, I bade farewell to the Pakistan Military Academy and my career as a soldier. I was very sad. It was not until my wife and I and all the dogs and luggage were aboard the coastal steamer leaving Karachi that my mood lightened. Ahead of me lay a new life in business in the mercantile world of Bombay – and, though I didn't know it then, eventual settlement in the United States of America.

20

Two Dozen Red Roses

I have always been one for the ladies, as they say. They have given me much happiness and pleasure. Leaving aside the feminine attraction, which on occasion I have found irresistible, I simply like being in the company of women. I like men per se, and I have had many exhilarating experiences in the company of my peers; this is particularly true of my days in action in World War II, and while founding the Pakistan Military Academy. However, if I had the choice, I would far rather spend an evening, or a day in the country for that matter, with an attractive, intelligent woman. Aside from the conversation and camaraderie, there is the satisfaction of being able to gaze at a beautiful face or figure, or both. Obviously this attraction has led to both good and bad involvements. I have been 'through the hoop,' i.e. divorced, a couple of times. I am not going to cast stones, but my second marriage was a real bust. It occurred just after World War II, and I think I was a bit dingy; probably the lady was too. Anyway, it was less than a success and after I had resigned my commission and was living in Bombay, we had a semi-agreeable parting and the lady left for England.

Living the life of a temporary bachelor, I was able to indulge my preference for female company, and I am more than grateful to a number of very charming ladies who brightened that period of my life. I must admit that not all of these delightful companions were unmarried. This added additional spice to life and some excitement, one suspicious husband hiring a private eye to tail me, and persuading one of the lady's other (unknown to him, but not to me) admirers to pay me a 'friendly' and unannounced visit to my flat to check the whereabout of said lady. Luckily I got news of the visit and the lady had already left for my other little menage. Keeps one young, so they say.

Inevitably, however, I fell in love. The lady in question, whom I still adore, was unfortunately married to someone else. Her husband worked on Sundays and so, with his blessing, it became routine for the two of us to rendezvous every Sunday at 5.30 am, before the heat of the day, and drive to Marve Beach where we picnicked, swam and sunbathed throughout the long tropical day and evening.

In those days Marve, some twenty-five miles north of Bombay, was little used by the foreign community, most of whom patronized Juhu Beach, only about twelve miles out. Marve Beach was really a small cove, an almost perfect half-mile crescent of gently rolling breakers and soft white sand. At one end a small point of rocks juts into the Arabian Sea. Here the pools left by the receding tide were full of anemones, sea urchins and small fish. A delightful place to wander hand-in-hand, surrounded by my three Australian terriers and the lady's spaniels.

A little further afield, to the north, was another rocky promontory, again full of tidal pools and grottoes. This area was not easy of access, and was not overlooked from the nearby fishing village. Here we found our grotto, sufficient overhang to give us shade and privacy, and a smooth rocky basin through which the waves swished back and forth, throughout the long tropical day. It was not surprising that we both fell deeply and irrevocably in love.

The summer and the following winter passed in a flash, with the lady's husband allowing us almost endless opportunities to meet. We both wondered where it all would end. About Christmas time there was a minor showdown. I had a party at my flat and the lady's husband, walking into my kitchen unannounced, found me kissing the back of his wife's neck as she bent over the stove. Hardly a passionate interlude, but he took grave exception, and expressed his displeasure by dropping about a dozen of my best plates which he was carrying at the time. Irritating but not irreplaceable. Obviously there had to be some explanation, and it seemed the moment to tell him that I had fallen in love with his wife. Other than the incident of the plates, there was no drama. He said he had guessed that we had become rather more than close friends, that he had applied to his company for a transfer to England and, until their departure in a couple of months, he forbade us to see one another except on a purely social basis. Of course we managed to meet, but not as frequently or as easily as before. Both of us were deeply distressed but agreed to keep in touch.

I arranged to take a long leave in England. I arrived there about a month after the lady. A week with my wife revealed that all was over between us and we agreed to separate. I spent my time between my brother's house in

Sussex and my club in London. For a long time I had no direct contact with the lady. Then one day the phone rang in Sussex. She said, 'G. and I have not been getting on at all well, and I have told him I must see you. He has agreed to my going to London for a week. Will you meet me?' Can a duck swim? I said, 'Of course, darling, I long to see you, but what brought this on? Has he agreed to us meeting?' 'Yes. He feels that if we see one another again in a fresh environment, we may decide we are not meant for one another.' How ingenuous can some people be? 'When are you coming?' 'Today. Can you meet me at Euston Station (London) on the 5.15 from Liverpool?' I was ecstatic. 'I shall be there, long before five!'

Just behind my club on Piccadilly, in Hertford Street, is a block of service flats which I have used periodically for years. I rang the owners and booked a flat for a week. Alas, the week passed all too quickly. We had a heavenly time dining, dancing and going to the theatre. At the end we were more in love than ever, if that were possible. We were also uncertain what was the right thing to do; there were a lot of ties to be cut, and then there would be a lot of loose ends to tie up. We agreed to let things rest for a while and see how the situation developed.

I took off on a business trip to Scandinavia. When I returned a month later, I went to stay with my brother at Cuckfield. He and his wife had been kind enough to invite my teenage daughter and son for the weekend. It was 13 October. The phone rang at 10.00 am. It was the lady calling long distance from her home in Cheshire. 'Darling, I've had it. I've decided to leave G.' This was the prelude. After many difficulties and chasing about, we found our way and still celebrate the anniversary of 13 October with two dozen red roses.

I started this episode with the statement that I had 'been through the hoop' a couple of times. There are places in my story where I have rather casually referred to 'my wife' or a lady's name. I thought I should be more explicit in that both ladies referred to had, at times, considerable influence on my actions and decisions.

Over the period of Partition and while at Kakul, I was married to Heather. In fact we were married in my house at Kakul in 1949. We separated in Bombay in 1956, and I married Margaret there the following year. I am very happy to record that over thirty years later, Margaret and I are still happily married, and it was she who accompanied me on our State visit to Pakistan in 1982.

21

Pakistani Postscript

In the spring of 1982 I was resting a gouty foot after attending the funeral of an old friend. Before putting my throbbing foot to rest, I paid a visit to my mailbox. Resting atop the usual pile of junk mail was a letter, 'On Her Majesty's Service', originating in the office of the British Military Attaché in Islamabad.

Very intrigued, I returned to my bed and tore open the envelope. It was from the Attaché, Brigadier Dellum, informing me that the President of Pakistan General Mohammed Zia-ul-Haq, in his capacity as Chief of Staff of the Army, was proposing to issue an invitation to my wife and myself to visit Pakistan as state guests for five weeks during the months of September and October, 1982. While the primary object was for me to attend the September Passing Out Parade at the Pakistan Military Academy, the formal invitation would also state that we might elect to travel anywhere in Pakistan we chose. Brigadier Dellum asked for a list of such places and our assurance that we would be able to accept the invitation.

I rushed down to our local 'village' – Tiburon, California – to contact my wife at her shop, The Royal Enclosure. Naturally she greeted me with 'What are you doing out of bed?' I thrust the letter upon her. We looked at each other, speechless and overcome with happiness, and also, in my case, with nostalgia. It was over thirty years since I had relinquished my command at Kakul. I dashed off a cable and a follow-up letter indicating the places we would like to visit in addition to the PMA.

I had started my army career in 1929 iin the Khyber Pass at the frontier post of Landi Kotal, so that was my first choice. Next I also wanted to visit

Peshawar, the state of Swat Sargodha Remount Depot and Jhelum where my late regiment, the 6th Lancers, was currently stationed. Obviously Rawalpindi, Islamabad and Karachi would be included.

In due course the official invitation arrived and on 3rd September we were on our way. Everything was first class—literally; I began to realize what this meant when we touched down in Paris and a Captain in the Pakistan Navy insisted on carrying my small overnight bag! Two days of great comfort and sightseeing at the Hilton Hotel overlooking the River Seine and we were on our way again, overnight to Karachi. Here, in the morning, we landed and were met by the Station Commander, an old polo-playing friend, and the officers who were to be my aides throughout the visit. The principal of these was Lieutenant-Colonel Rahim of the Baluch Regiment. On to Rawalpindi where we were housed in regal splendour in the presidential suite on the top floor of the modern Intercontinental Hotel.

Rawalpindi Mall with the Officers' Club and its seedy bungalows looked much the same as I remembered it in the 1930s. The Saddar Bazaar had not changed much either. My old tailor's grandson came to pay his respects to me and kindly made me a khaki bush jacket with new medal ribbons for my visit to the 6th Lancers. In the 1930s G.M. Abdul Aziz made the best polo breeches in what was then Northern India; now the firm was still doing business from the same pokey little shops in the Saddar, and with the same perfection.

Soon after arrival I paid a visit to the new capital, Islamabad, to call upon the United States and British Ambassadors. I was amazed at the growth of vegetation in the capital's surroundings – lush undergrowth and trees everywhere. In the 1930s I remember picnicking at the Rawal Pool and shooting partridge in this area. Then it was a barren rocky expanse, sparesely covered with a few thorn trees; today it reminded me of the area surrounding Washington DC, all thanks to the flow of water from the great dams built to the north.

Before we left Rawalpindi we received an invitation to dine with the President, General Zia-ul-Haq, at the Army Chief of Staff's residence; this was where the General preferred to live, rather than the more pretentious presidential residence in Islamabad.

A staff car picked us up from our hotel. When we arrived, most of the guests were congregated on the lawn in front of the building. There were about twenty-four in all, senior members of the Government and their wives. Many of them were friends from long ago. It was a great pleasure for us to mingle with them and chat about the early days of Pakistan. After a while, the President and Begum Zia-ul-Haq came out from the house and we chatted for a while before dinner. The dinner was formal and of course there was no wine. All the ladies were seated on one side of the table and all the men on the other – an unusual but attractive idea in some ways. Pakistani ladies are not very forthcoming in public, but Margaret, who sat among them, was able to keep up a continual talk across the table with the President and other male guests opposite her. After dinner, the President rose and proposed my health. He followed this courtesy with a most fulsome speech about my services to the Pakistan Army and referred to me as 'one of the founding fathers of the Army'. Finally he handed me a parchment appointing me his Honorary Consul-General in California, duly signed by himself and his Foreign Minister. This, coupled with his remarks, was in most gracious recognition of my achievements at Kakul so long ago.

The next few days were spent in a visit to the 6th Lancers. They could not have been more hospitable and they included a large group of pensioners, mostly bearded and sere – I hardly recognized my personal radio operator of 1944 in Italy, he looked so aged; long retired as a *Risaldar*, he was living out his declining years in his village in the Salt Range. Luncheon in the officers' mess was nostalgic, surrounded by mementoes of over a hundred years ago which I had viewed for the first time when I joined the regiment in 1929. The history of some of the items had been lost; but in a few cases I was able to bring my successors up to date. Colonel V. M. Stockley's record elephant tusk was still in its place above the anteroom fireplace, resting below a signed portrait of the late Queen Mary. I felt as though I were joining the Regiment all over again.

Then there was a visit to Lahore at the invitation of the Governor of the Punjab: more huge receptions and greetings from many more old friends. Thence to Peshawar, where we were received by the Governor of the North West Frontier and stayed and were royally entertained in Government House. Lieutenant-General Fazl-i-Haq, the Governor, had been one of my cadets at Kakul in 1948. I was proud to note that, out of the four Pakistani provinces, three of them were now being governed by ex-cadets of mine. Incidentally, many of Pakistan's Ambassadors abroad were also at one time cadets of my regime, including the Ambassador to the United States of America, Lieutenant-General Ejaz Azeem.

It was while I was staying at GH in Peshawar that I had a surprising and very happy reunion – with the old *dhobi* who had remained at Kakul when every other Hindu fled to India, and whom I had taken on as my household washerman. After I left he had moved to Peshawar, where one of the Governor's predecessors had given him continuing sanctuary and a job at GH. After all the inter-religious mayhem of Partition, it was heart-warming to find this aged Hindu still alive and living safely and honourably in the house of a Moslem.

Before we left Pakistan we spent a day in the Khyber, escorted by the Political Agent to the area. It was a lovely day as we wound up the twists and turns of the famous Pass, but I noticed quite a few changes. The railway was the same as ever, the camel road was deserted – no caravans with their hundreds of swaying beasts, dogs, donkeys and wide-eyed children, which had been a feature of the days when I lived at Landi Kotal. And the motor road was full of traffic: huge trucks laden with merchandise passed backwards and forwards between Peshawar and Kabul – despite the ongoing occupation of Afghanistan by the Soviets. My old encampment no longer existed. There was no regular brigade in the Pass now; the security lay in the hands of the Khyber Rifles, located in small posts dotted about the countryside. I inspected the Khyber Rifles' guard at Torkham, the actual frontier post opposite the Russian/Afghan post. As we drove back up the Pass I was happy to see that all the British regimental badges, carved in the rocky hillside, were well preserved as honourable relics of the British Raj.

Later we returned to Peshawar and spent an evening in the depths of the city. This was where I had bought my first cigarette container in 1929: a delightful circular silver holder for a fifty-cigarette pack, embossed with little goddesses, which I had watched being hammered out by a Hindu silversmith. And we visited 'Poor Ali', of course; his shop has been patronized by most of the crowned heads of the world and others such as Jacqueline Kennedy – he has pictures and signatures to prove his widespread popularity. We bought some Russian pottery, the famous Gardiner pottery that originated in St Petersburg in the early part of the century. Gardiner was a Scot who settled in Russia and designed beautiful pottery in distinctive colours. These pieces were distributed throughout the Muslim areas of Russia, as well as Afghanistan and the northern parts of India. Because of the acceptance of his wares in these Muslim areas he signed every piece in the Urdu script, which read (phonetically) 'Gardner'. Today they are still known by this name and we were able to find some precious pieces.

After a final reception and dinner to which yet more old friends were invited, we flew by PIA to Saidu Sharif in the beautiful valley of Swat. For a couple of happy days we were entertained by Prince Aurungzeb of Swat and his wife, and also had the pleasure of dining with his father, the ex-Wali of Swat, Jahanzeb, who had long been a friend of mine. The next day we departed by helicopter for the Military Academy, Kakul. This entailed taking off at about 3500 feet and negotiating a series of some seven or eight ridges over 10,000 feet each. The helicopter was grossly overloaded with a crew of four, our party of three and a lot of baggage; but at last, after a lot of huffing and puffing, we made it and entered the Abbottabad Valley.

As the helicopter turned across the Abbottabad cantonment we saw some buildings ahead of us, at the top of a long lane of poplars which I had planted so long ago. The buildings had sprung up over the intervening years, and for a moment I was disorientated. But, as the chopper swung around, I got my bearings. The first thing I recognized was a weather-beaten sign outside the Academy Convocation Hall: erected by my colleagues thirty-five years ago, it still read: 'The Ingall Hall'. I had thought it would long have gone, perhaps superseded by a more Islamic name. After landing, the Commandant told me that the Government had decided to build a new hall but that it should continue to bear my name. I have never been more proud or gratified.

That night I met many of my old friends: the squash marker (pro), my old gardener and many others. In the evening there was a large reception at the Commandant's House, comprising many of those who had served on my staff. They had even sent for my old bearer, Adalat Khan, from the mountains of Azad Kashmir. I could not have had a more delightful reunion. Next day the passing out parade was excellent; the drill would have been outstanding even on Horse Guards Parade in London.

Finally we left loaded with gifts, for Karachi and thence via London to the United States. Soon after my return the President of Pakistan, General Zia-ul-Haq, paid a state visit to the United States. I flew to Washington DC to greet him and attended the formal dinner in his honour. Among the three hundred people who sat down to dine that night were the Vice President of the United States and Mrs Bush, Cabinet members and many other distinguished personages. General Zia rose to speak, and after a while I suddenly realized that he was speaking of me. He was most gracious and warm in his remarks, referring to me again as 'one of the founding fathers of our Army'. It took him more than five minutes to recount what he considered my more significant services to Pakistan in the early days. Finally he said: 'I know the Brigadier is here. Brigadier Ingall, will you please stand up.' This I did and was given a standing ovation by the assembled guests.

After dinner, as I was leaving, I encountered the Foreign Minister of Pakistan, Lieutenant-General Sahabzads Yakub Khan, in the foyer of the hotel. The Minister was a fellow cavalryman, having been posted to the 18th Cavalry on first commission; later, after the inception of Pakistan, he had commanded my old regiment, the 6th Lancers. I told him that I had found General Zia's remarks at dinner most gracious and moving, and asked him to convey my great appreciation to the General.

Putting his arm around my shoulder he said, 'Bingle, you are never going to be forgotten in Pakistan – and moreover you are very greatly loved.'

This I considered the ultimate compliment and the final word on my years at the Pakistan Military Academy – and it was most fitting in that it was spoken by an officer who had been one of my successors as Commander of the 6th Lancers.

Last Post

Even now, in the 1980s, my thoughts often return to those days: my life as Commandant of the Pakistan Military Academy, the partitioning of British India before that, and – still further back – my life as a Bengal Lancer.

I relive those heady moments in Italy, that exhilarating gallop through the plains of Lombardy in April 1945 and my last day of fighting as a professional soldier. I recall the thrill of going out on manoeuvres while stationed at Sialkot. But above all I can never forget the excitement of those earliest days of my career, when I was still a young officer, so fresh out of Sandhurst and England and now with the cavalry on the Kajauri plain.

It was only a small triumph perhaps, in the greater scheme of things, but for me that charge on the Afridi hordes at the Samgakki Pass, when I was only twenty-two, will remain a precious memory for ever. Sitting atop my horse, at the head of sixty or so troopers, and drawing my sword while the men aimed their lances at the bold tribesmen in our path . . . Those really were the last days of the Bengal Lancers.

154

Index